NOW IS YOUR LAST CHANCE

NOW
IS YOUR
LAST
CHANCE

**End All Suffering and Confusion
and Awaken to Your True Purpose**

ISSE

Now is Your Last Chance / Ismet "Isse" Muratspahic
ISBN 978-91-987261-0-7

1. Awareness. 2. Self-actualization (Psychology).
3. Spiritual life.

Published in Sweden by
Temsy Of Sweden AB
www.temsy.se

Cover photo by Artem Militonian/Unsplash
Cover design & typesetting by Haris Tucakovic

"Rooted in his deep personal experience, Isse gives us the clear roadmap to awakening that we didn't know we needed so badly. In powerful and direct language, we are guided to recognize and acknowledge our own inherent wisdom and not to settle for anything less."

Alex Greene
Founder of Red Beard Somatic Therapy

This book is written for you,
by your true self,
one you yet
may not know.

"Nothing is true before it's experientially true for you.
Now is the time to reclaim what was always yours."
—Isse

TABLE OF CONTENTS

The Night is Dark

Although I rarely think about my past experiences, more commonly referred to as my "life story," I would like to share with you a pivotal, transformational moment that irreversibly changed the course of my whole life. Consider my sharing of this experience to be an inspirational invitation to navigate your life experience consciously – from now on.

I had just entered my thirties and found myself in an increasingly uncomfortable and painful predicament. Like most of the human, I did my very best to sedate and control this discomfort by increasing the effort I put into activities, relationships, and all other socially acceptable substances in order to find my purpose and to make some sense of my life experience. However, underneath all these activities, conversations, relationships, and places, I had a deep sense that something was fundamentally wrong. The subtle message was, "This can't be it."

This part of me where the message dwelled seemed to be constantly present, once visible, and it was always showing up with this message when I least wanted it to. Typically, when something externally went according to my plan and I felt that I finally deserved harmony, this undesirable state would show itself and crash my party. Since at the time, I considered the message to be negative and harmful, I also decided it was evil. For the person I considered myself to be, the message was also deeply annoying. I had done my utmost externally and mentally up to this point, by studying and applying myself to whatever path was presented in order to find happiness. This approach certainly manifested successes in the external world with considerable financial progress as I rapidly moved to the very top of the corporate ladder. I thought I would deeply enjoy the lifestyle that came along with such a predicament with its fancy titles, beautiful homes and luxury vacations. Nevertheless, this socially imprinted fairytale never gave me the harmony I had been promised it would, and I was instead thrown into even deeper internal conflicts around my life experience.

Wherever I sought salvation and help, I was shown a direction that left me disempowered and disappointed. Life seemed so raw, and I felt left alone in the quicksand. Wherever I moved, with the best intentions, I only seemed to sink deeper into confusion and despair. By this point, depression and anxiety up to a level of total paralysis had been my everyday life for years. After numerous conscious and unconscious attempts to check out of my life experience, I found myself stuck in a deep paradox of despair; I didn't want to die, but I just didn't want to live.

One night, like numerous others, I was lying alone in my physically comfortable bed, and I was shaking, drowning in a seemingly unexplainable deep-rooted hole of fear. The silence was unbearable to my mind, and at this particular moment the increasing feeling of despair seemed to have no end, no climax; the pit into which I was falling was bottomless. The frontier between thought and reality dissolved, and my mind habitually did its utmost to assist me into what I, in that moment, happily considered to be the comfort of high-level anxiety. That salvation didn't occur, however; instead, my whole body started to shake vigorously as my mental activity simultaneously went to its absolutely full potential to try to analyze and explain this experience. The intensity and pressure just escalated and reached a height where I began to prepare myself for death.

For a split second that felt like eternity, I surrendered to death just before, as if from a nightmare, all the built-up energetic force catapulted me up and I shouted out – "I don't know!" Suddenly, a vast emptiness filled my whole being and my mind, which, probably for the first time in my life, became totally silent. I found myself just sitting silently in bed while something with a soft voice from a deep state of my being, not reachable or intellectually explainable, whispered – "I know."

While this message was delivered, my body underwent a radical energetic shift and I became filled with a warm sensation as I was gently pushed back into a horizontal position. The totality of the experience wasn't a thought, a physical sensation nor a feeling – it was a state of being. This state took me radically into what felt like a limitless hug of unconditional love. I lay there, staring at the ceiling with tears in my eyes. Overwhelmed. I had never felt so loved, so welcome, so at home. An undoubtable truth was communicated from this state of being: that my life as I knew it, and all the accompanying suffering to this point, was over now. What baffled my mind and made it undoubtedly agree to this truth was the fact that all of my desires had been answered and met in this state of being – instantly.

That night, the Being asked me to follow two simple principles in order to access a relationship with the infinite all-knowing. The first one was to follow unconditionally whatever was shown to be true, and the second was to share this truth. Being a depressed businessman and an avid advocate of "pacta sunt servanda" (agreements must be kept) at that point, I signed up immediately. Now was my last chance.

This experience allowed me to embark on an almost decade-long journey home, and the book you are holding is the gift of wisdom that I have received from developing an intimate relationship with our shared Being. Later, I learned that the experience I had was commonly described in ancient teachings as the appearance of "night visitors" – past energies that arrive to wake us up to our true selves through a total collapse of the ego.

The journey directly after my awakening experience started out blissfully. The morning after, birds stopped shouting and I intensely noticed that the birds were actually singing. Being didn't ask me to change any particular external circumstances; I was simply asked to be the qualities of the present moment in the same set of external circumstances, and this fundamentally transformed the whole perception of my life experience – which ultimately started transforming anyone who entered my sphere. In the external world, this shift made others question whether I were constantly in love. And surely, I was dwelling in love.

A couple of years later, Being started to progressively move me into stillness by rearranging my external circumstances until I was more or less in solitude. I was gently called to quit my high-paying job, move to a smaller city, and withdraw my energy from more or less all previous relationships and material possessions, until I found myself having a life experience where I was simply walking and sitting on benches. Now, my new job was simply to be. There weren't many in my external environment who understood or supported my new job, and the shifts were surely confusing for periods, even to me, but I had promised to listen and follow. A promise is a promise, and this love was undoubtedly worth dying for. Awakening is a spectacular miracle for a small audience.

During these years, I was spontaneously called to take short notes as an increasing number of individuals started to reach out for my guidance. Then, one day, I intuitively started the writing of this text and was called to structure it in its purest form with the original questions and answers.

This book is structured as a road map that points to a journey that is typically referred to as an awakening or enlightenment. This is the process whereby we are moved through the trinity of finding, knowing, and finally being ourselves. Once we commit to this quest, all resources of the universe automatically line up perfectly to support our journey home and to move us in alignment with our form's true purpose in this world. This is where we will forever and instantly find all internal and external richness for which we search.

Let it Be Light

It's no coincidence that you, at this particular time, are holding this book. You are holding it and reading these words because your soul asked you to do it. Another way to put it is that your subconscious asks you lovingly to wake up from unconsciousness – consciously. You have been longing for something that, at this point, you may not yet be able to articulate or know through your own experience. You may feel lost or let down by life, or you may simply have a curiosity for something beyond your current boundaries and perception of life. You may be suffering and feel deep hopelessness and despair.

No matter what your previous or current life experience may be, there's a part of you that resonates with the idea that everything will be all right. In fact, everything is already all right – right now. There's a part of you that knows this to be true, even if your current moment may be veiled by the intensity of experience. Nothing real can ever be lost – it may simply be veiled. We can at any moment unveil it by exposing it to the truth, or the light. The light will eternally dissolve anything that is exposed to it or shown to be untrue. Exposing something to the light is the same as being deeply aware of it on all levels of our Being. Since no one can put attention on awareness on behalf of someone else, I can't give you the truth, but what I can do with these words is to point you towards it.

Only you can give yourself the gift of eternal joy and life. This is your free will, by design. It is also your birthright and responsibility to reclaim what was always yours: your total freedom.

The sole meaning of this book is to point you to an experience through which you ought to develop an intimate relationship with our shared Being in order to reveal and live your life expression's purpose, purposely.

When this is accomplished – everything is accomplished.

I am forever grateful for all the lessons put in front of me by my parents, grandparents, and all conscious teachers I have encountered. More importantly, I am grateful for the gift of life itself. This book is collectively written by everyone who has entered my life experience to this point, generations before, and then beyond that. In that sense, these are our teachings – a gathering of simple pointers to remember the totality and simplicity of what we already are. It's a gathering of words in a specific order that aim to point you to the truth of human experience and beyond. All words should be considered knowledge, and at best a belief pending verification within your own laboratory, which is your life experience. Once experientially verified, they will become your wisdom. When you start to live by this wisdom, you will discover peace, joy and your true purpose in this life and world. Then you will embark on an eternal journey called the celebration of life itself. May you climb until the mountains disappear.

Thank you – for Being you.

Love,
Isse

The Spell of Words

If at any time you experience overwhelm upon reading this text, or simply observe yourself skimming through it rapidly, I urge you to stop reading and connect with your inner body by taking a couple of deep and conscious breaths. Remind yourself that there's no hurry and that your destiny is perfectly tailored for your soul's highest potential. Look around at your current surroundings and feel the deep vibration of life. Feel how important this present moment is. Feel how important you are, for all of us, for taking this journey home. Feel how, by embracing this present moment, by digesting the experience of this text, you are ultimately changing the course of all of your future present moments. Feel how you already are, whole and complete, in your pure quest to take the journey home. There is no destination that is purer and more beautiful than the love of the quest itself.

Although language and words are neutral in themselves, they do become limited in terms of the meanings we assign to them based on our social and cultural imprinting. Therefore, all words should only be used as pointers towards an experience and should always be examined within your own life experience. We want the spell of words and the assignment of the meaning to be pointing us to an open-ended investigating experience that benefits us – not towards one that blocks and puts a spell on us.

When the word *mind* is used throughout this text, it points to the totality of our perceived experience within the field of our awareness. Mind includes not only our thoughts, but all perceptions, such as physical and emotional expressions. When it's necessary to point to a specific dimension within our mind, terminology such as mental body, physical body, emotional body and inner body are also used. Mental body is all energies that contain our mental activity – which is the same as our thoughts. Inner body is the awakening experience we have when we put our attention on the inner energy field of our physical body.

I prefer to use the word Being or your True Self when I point to the universal all-knowing experience within you. Occasionally, I use the words Presence, Divine, Love, Creator, Higher Self or God. Ultimately, if you find one – you find all. All teachings aim to point us towards the same experience. I use the word God sporadically since it carries a lot of imprinted generational and geographical baggage across our planet. For many of us, this word may create unnecessary disturbance on the mental plane with endless discussions around this experience. Ultimately, this experience can never be mentally understood but only felt as a state of being. Our task is not to argue about mental fairytales about God; our task is to go deep into our life experience and to first find out and then *know* for ourselves what the experience of our Being is, and how our life experience is affected when we operate from this deeper dimension of ourselves. All words should be considered gentle pointers towards the experience of emptiness itself, and I suggest that you choose those words that have as small a predetermined charge or meaning as possible based on your situation. We can't afford to waste our energy on the mental level of thought when we aim to dwell in a state of Being which, once we have awakened, we will refer to as heaven on earth.

Simultaneously, when it comes to the experience we perceive when we are operating from the dimension of our personalized small self, which is a cocktail of beliefs that are held together by past physical sensations, thoughts, emotions, actions and all other absorbed experiences, I usually refer to it as the ego, personalized self or imprinted self.

Throughout the text, the word *energy* is commonly used to refer to a movement within our field of awareness. Energy points towards all movement and not exclusively to our emotions. Hence, physical sensations, and thought patterns that we perceive within the borders of our human experience are included in the word energy.

Furthermore, although this text is structured in a specific order resembling a road map, it ultimately points towards the experience of oneness in Being present. Therefore, it's appropriate to share that the experiential phases we encounter are not a linear process since we are operating in a timeless paradigm. They very much overlap, and the sole meaning of the structure is to give us sufficient mental clarity based on our predicament in order to move beyond any perceived barriers. Therefore, different words, structures and pointers are used based on the consciousness level from which the questions arise. The text may also come across as repetitive or contradictory for your restless mental body, and I therefore urge you to be compassionate with yourself when digesting this content. Deeper layers are first revealed once we digest one level of our experience. Hence, we aim to develop eternal patience with ourselves.

Why did you even write this book if the experience we're searching for can't be put into words?

Simply put, because we lose ourselves through repetition and we remember ourselves through repetition. We ought to experience and consciously feel every word in our hearts as if we are meeting it for the first time. And when we are conscious, the experience is that we are meeting it for the first time. Like a manual, all words are simply pointers that bring novelty to how to observe our life experience from a higher and deeper dimension of ourselves. Once you have the experience, all words are redundant.

This is confusing to me; you're talking about an experience that can't be talked about.

I know that the paradox may be annoying at this stage, but knowing, through experience, the potential and limitations of different levels of your being will dissolve all paradoxes. Awareness of this statement alone is already a first step to the dissolution of this particular conflict. The validity of any experience is in the awareness of the experience itself. The devil may be in the details, but so are the angels.

You write about moving beyond – what do you mean by that?

To move beyond a phenomenon is simply to keep looking further, deeper, and broader. We move beyond by allowing that level of experience to be as it is. We move beyond by observing the experience as we meet it for the first time. We move beyond by asking questions about the experience without entertaining a predetermined mental answer. We move beyond through the realization that either we will get the answer, or our need to keep asking the question will dissolve. We move beyond by including the experience as a part of the whole. We move beyond by letting the movement be on all levels. We move beyond without entertaining the need to mentally understand what moving beyond means, because moving beyond is at first a feeling, then a state of Being. By feeling the resonance of truth in this statement, you have moved beyond your mental image about this statement. Ultimately, we know that we have moved beyond when we choose, by the grace of acceptance, to move beyond.

PART I

FINDING YOURSELF

Movement beyond conflicting thinking

"Never argue with yourself; whoever wins, you lose."

Now is Our Last Chance

Human beings get confused when we don't know from our true experience how to navigate this ship we call life. Simultaneously, we lose ourselves in all sorts of attachments and desires due to first our incapability, then our unwillingness to embrace the present moment where true navigation resides. When acting out this illusion, we give in to all sorts of egoistic desires that cloud our life experience with suffering. This strengthens the egoistic belief in false self, and the vast consequence is that we stop trusting our own inherited ability to navigate our being authentically.

We stop trusting ourselves, and not trusting our true self is the same as agreeing to live within an existential crisis in this world. The ego won't at any cost acknowledge this truth and instead catapults us into further external action in order to give us some sense of relief and safety. We then typically turn away from our inner being and get entangled in endless activities, relationships, and conversations in order to try to find some relief on the mental plane. These activities both fragment and disorientate us – which is the same as being lost.

We act based on the illusion that we are confused by accepting the thought as valid. We do this when we first believe and consequently behave according to our thought patterns. Our inability to have a sorted and clear mental body makes us act out the lowest level of our energetic capabilities, also called our thoughts. Thought is the lowest form of truth, and its sole purpose is to navigate *what* we aim to do. Thought can't solve *why* we ought to do it. These deeper levels of our being are extracted from the stillness in the present moment and are only available to us when we are still.

Furthermore, the route of navigating purely based on thought makes human beings, on a collective level, the most afraid and confused beings in the universe as we know it. We are afraid of everything. We are afraid of love, we are afraid of hate, we are afraid of life, we are afraid of death, we are afraid of darkness, and we are afraid of the light. No other being on this planet carries so much psychological resistance and self-inflicted conflict towards life itself than we do. We are also one of the most vulnerable beings on this planet; a human child needs extensive care from its parents, considering both frequency and length of care, compared to basically all other beings.

This vulnerability frustrates us to such a level that we mis-use the true potential of our being. The consequence is that we are mis-navigating our being by self-inflicting judgment and pain, both on ourselves and others.

The consequences of human unconsciousness have, in various shapes and forms, haunted mankind for thousands and thousands of years. We have done our utmost to fight this dilemma through the creation of laws, religions, borders, and nations. Throughout history, it seems that for as much justice as we manage to bring to one place on our planet, an equal amount of disturbance and conflict pops up in another part of the world.

There seems to be no end to our suffering. Even if all of our efforts have, in some areas and during certain periods of our evolvement, given us a perception of control and relief, both globally and as a species, human beings have not managed to bring a totality of harmonization to our common life experience.

However, the solution is simple, obvious, and instantly available to all of us. On an individual level, we all have both a responsibility and an opportunity to bring instant harmony to the whole, by bringing about instant harmony within ourselves. This is our birthright and free will, by design. In this sense, now, the present moment, is always our last chance for salvation.

Why are We Suffering

The first Noble Truth in the Buddhist tradition is that all life is suffering. This refers to human life experience when navigated exclusively from our small, personalized self. Mankind has for many thousands of years tried to address the problem of human suffering, so the phenomenon that human experience is clouded with imbedded confusion is nothing new.

However, human beings' investment in mental and technological evolvement has accelerated the consequences of our suffering. This refers to how we perceive both our internal and external life experience. Everything is accelerating in this time and age while our organism has had very limited time to adjust to these shifts. This is evident by the state of our planet and the simple fact that we rarely encounter anyone in modern societies who is genuinely happy with their life experience. We perceive an increased level of uncertainty, chaos, and meaninglessness in our internal experience that is occurring simultaneously with increased levels of natural disasters, pandemics, and conflict in our external experience.

We both move and change work more frequently, and our mind is exposed to an increased number of impressions and attachments in our lifespan. We struggle to maintain meaningful relationships, and while we are in them, we are utterly afraid that they will end. And since we have lost our ability to fully commit to ourselves, and hence to others, this abandonment is precisely what we manifest in a fearful repetitive loop. We have lost the ability to trust ourselves and others.

We have a higher degree of options and a higher level of expectations regarding what we ought to accomplish during a lifetime. The increased number of attachments and expectations simply means accumulation of more disruption to continuity in our life experience. We experience both increased and more rapid changes. Since all change is an ending to something, this is the same as stating that we are experiencing an increased amount of grief. Simultaneously, we spend little to no effort and time on digesting these experiences by embracing and processing the changes by consciously drawing wisdom from them in the present moment. We rather apply a "hit-and-run" distraction strategy by moving our attention away from what is actually happening in the present moment. Unfortunately, this strategy has a fundamental long-term consequence that is the root of all our suffering: *identification with the thought by resisting the present moment.* All these accumulated and unfinished energetic states of grief don't magically vanish simply because we distract our attention with a new experience or activity. This energy is instead dysfunctionally transformed into another mind state, where it usually manifests as a confused and agitated mental body. One way this unresolved grief manifests in our life experience is as various states of hostility, anxiety, worry and disrupted sleep patterns.

Our mind is exposed to a never-ending input of information in various formats and channels from all over our planet – *instantly and constantly.* Even if we have not been previously imprinted with a fearful past, we imprint ourselves endlessly by absorbing collectively created fear. Simultaneously, since we don't have the ability to digest and process all this information in such an accelerated manner, we need to shut down by distracting ourselves in order to escape total overwhelm. Since we don't consciously take a stand by embracing these energies in the present moment, our mind instinctively and primitively draws conclusions from this information unconsciously. Underneath, no matter if we admit it or not, we feel threatened and unsafe.

This collectively absorbed and unprocessed fear creates internal agreements and beliefs around how we need to think, feel and behave in order to create a sense of safety in this world. These internally upheld agreements and beliefs create what we typically call the personalized small self, or the ego. *The amount of unprocessed and denied past experiences is proportionate to the amount of ego we need to entertain in order to feel protected in our life experience.*

However, the solution to this devastating situation is both simple and effortless: to move beyond suffering is to first realize that resistance to our perceived pain is the actual suffering itself. By moving beyond this resistance to life itself, we move beyond suffering. Movement beyond suffering is completed once we surrender to what is – as it is. We simply need to be fully present in order to dissolve all the suffering of the world. Now, the present moment, is always our last chance for salvation.

I want to save the planet; isn't that a good intention in order to alleviate suffering?

We ought to be honest with ourselves and therefore with others, and not to misdirect our intentions toward what we perceive to be the suffering of the planet. We say that we want to save the planet when we actually mean that we want to save ourselves. The planet is, and always will be, just fine as it is. The climate of the planet is not wrong just because human beings can't survive in such conditions. This simply means that our attention is misdirected away from solving our actual issue, which is, and always has been, human unconsciousness. We have had, and still have, perfect conditions to respond consciously to what is.

The modern human being becomes utterly confused when we misuse the deep potential of our being by overlooking simple logic and getting lost in our mental body – or our thoughts. We build societies and environments with core beliefs around inherited lack, and then we fight this predicament via misplaced intentions, such as *we must save the planet*. If we truly want to save the planet, we ought to save ourselves first. We can only alleviate the suffering of the planet by alleviating the suffering of our own life experience. That quest alone will save everything and everyone, forever.

Ego

Firstly, ego is neither good nor bad – it's neutral. Ego simply is. Ego isn't something that we need to fight or overcome. This is both impossible and counterproductive since we would by that tactic simultaneously create more ego to overcome the initial rise of an egoistic trait. It's easy to see the logic that a hammer can't strike itself and how this division would create more conflict within us. Identifying and acting upon this type of ego division also strengthens the underlying imprinted belief of shame that something is broken within us. *Nothing is nor has ever been broken.* We are all born innocent and perfectly harmonious, and no experience we have had or might have can change this universal fact regarding our true self.

This doesn't mean that our imprinting or experiences don't have a considerable impact on the intensity of our current life experience, but know that all experiences can be embraced and put to rest by taking refuge in the present moment, which is the home of our true self.

On a deeper level, you know this to be true. Our Being is built to survive any experience – no matter what the ego's own limitations based on past experiences might suggest currently. It's more accurate to say that ego is a trait that arises within our awareness that we are uncovering and discovering by putting our attention on observing it with our true self. Our true self is the same as awareness or consciousness. Therefore, we ought to cultivate an intention to embrace and learn, in our own experience, what our ego is, and what the consequences of identifying and operating from this limited level are.

Furthermore, ego is not an entity; it's simply a set of beliefs based on past experience that we have absorbed and used to draw limiting assumptions about life and our true self. When we uncover these experiences by non-judgmentally observing them, our egoistic beliefs are dismantled, and our true self, or the light, shines through. Therefore, we don't need to dissolve the ego. The ego dissolves itself when exposed to awareness.

Ego also hates its own job since it involves working constantly overtime to maintain a set of illusions, blocked energies and endless narratives about life without getting any playtime. *Being the ego is literally a never-ending story.* Since it's neither natural nor a light-filled way of living in accordance with the flow of life, ego is also very angry and blameful. Since we haven't discovered any other dimension from which we could operate and navigate life, we are also fearful of firing the ego from this dissatisfying job. It's the only reality we know, and on an instinctive level we do our utmost in order to survive. Therefore, when approaching our ego, we ought to be mindful of and thankful for what this dimension has done to this point in our life experience.

Shouldn't we just dismiss the ego since you state that it's just an illusion?

It's only an illusion if we know by experience who we are, and through this recognition, the ego's tricks are firstly exposed and then dissolved automatically. We shouldn't dismiss any egoistic counterstrikes to what is actually happening in the present moment. This includes all practices and techniques that aim to calm the mind. Such techniques are a denial of what is, which is the same as distraction and suppression based on fear.

If we have a hostile thought, we observe that thought until it dissolves from our field of awareness. We observe it deeply on all levels of our perceptive matrix. We observe how our physical posture, inner body sensations, and emotions are affected when we believe this thought to be true. We then ask ourselves: Is this thought pattern true under all circumstances? Suddenly, all sorts of past experiences and images pop up within our awareness that both support and dismiss this thought pattern. We are then witnessing the battle of the ego, which vividly tries to defend its own made-up positions based on internal agreements with roots in past experiences. We then put non-judgmental attention on subsequent inner body sensations that originate from these thought patterns.

Eventually, when the inner body charge connected to different egoistic beliefs is dismantled by feeling them through, the rise of this battle will appear just humorous. We will start to laugh about situations that would previously have gripped our perception and veiled our peace for weeks or months.

Therefore, it's more accurate to state that we are dissolving the ego by recognizing its limiting dimensions, rather than dismissing the ego through some sort of internal or external action. This is where we attain wisdom: through our own experience that the ego is literally a never-ending story. The ego is like a robotic puppy toy with a limiting, disruptive and repetitive repertoire, and our pure intention is simply to stop recharging its batteries.

Shouldn't I firstly calm the mind with meditation in order to be in emotional balance?

By all means, meditative practices can be very valuable in order to regulate our body-mind, although the intention behind any practice is the most fundamental dimension of any endeavor. Meditative and breathing practices with eyes closed are valuable, specifically if the authentic intention is to accumulate present moment awareness by physical stillness. This is a non-judgmental practice whereby we are open to whatever experience presents itself. It's a quest of discovery. With any other intentions, we are at risk of running ego's errands with a result-oriented approach. Even a well-meant intention to calm the mind is an activity based on a belief that we are the uncalm or broken mind.

Therefore, the most direct path is to stop with any intentions that aim to calm the mind, as this is impossible, counter-productive and strengthens the ego since calming the mind is the same as controlling the mind. We are at risk of becoming "spiritual" project managers of our mind. Our mind's expression mirrors our Being's qualities of energy, vibrancy and vivacity. Our aim is to unblock frozen energetic states and use that fuel to live our expression's purpose. We can't live our expression's purpose with a passive and controlled mind. Instead, we ought to observe the mind non-judgmentally, and it immediately starts to dissolve itself since it's just a set of beliefs that can't survive without us strengthening them with judgment or time-based results. Furthermore, we ought to trade the energy-consuming search for balance for the simplicity of surrendering to what is. We surrender to all experiences of life, and the gift we receive is far more significant than any balance: the experience of dwelling in everlasting harmony.

Fear and Hope

When we live an unconscious life, based on a false imprinted self, we are totally identified with the thought and the underlying charged energetic sensation. Within this paradigm we have no ability to be aware beyond the thought and to see further mechanics, or the play, within our field of awareness. In this setting, everything appears to be important and life-threatening. We lose the ability to distinguish the appropriate energy belonging to the present moment from the imprinting of the false self, or the ego, that drives the dysfunctional reactivity within the present moment when we perceive life through these dirty lenses. We don't have the ability to see past the energy field, and we become afraid of our own being. It's more accurate to say that we don't have the ability to *see past the past* within us. Most of the dysfunctional inner body sensations that we perceive in the present moment, and the negative thought patterns that derive primarily from the resistance to feeling these states, are unfinished experiences that have their roots in past experiences. We have imprinted ourselves with a habitual false belief that our inner body energy is in some way threatening and dangerous. We then escape and cut off the very energy that will liberate us, and that is our vehicle to the truth, commonly called our intuition. We mislabel important parts of our inner intelligent guiding principle as fear. Often, we loosely brand this experience as anxiety.

When we are unconscious, and these past experiences enter our field of awareness on the level of thoughts, we try to consciously balance them by creating a distinct counterstrike of mental hope. Hope is the group of dreams and fantasies we consciously force into our field of awareness in order to fight the unconscious thoughts that we don't want to meet in the present moment. Hope is a narrative about how some future moment will be more pleasant, and the creation of such a mental illusion provides a temporary lifting and a perception of softer energetic states within our inner body experience. We then temporarily settle for an illusion. This strategy is also commonly referred to as dissociation or escapism.

However, the consequence of navigating our life in such a way is conflict on various levels of our being, which ultimately ends in further confusion and suffering down the road. Sooner or later, we lose ourselves in conflicting hope narratives when the present moments throughout life don't resonate with these fantasies. We simply run out of stories to tell, and when this happens, ego will increasingly start to blame others and indulge in further self-inflicted victimization narratives.

We move beyond this predicament by realizing that our unconscious thought patterns in the present moment are primarily resistance towards feeling our inner body. Furthermore, the uncomfortable inner body experience in the present moment has a root in past experiences. That gives us a natural insight: *there's no such thing as a future – it's all past.* It's more accurate to say that resistance towards past energies is dysfunctionally converted in the present moment by our mental body to create a hope narrative that we call a future. The future is a fairytale about hope and dreams. The only authentic way to truly change the course of our future experience is by changing our relationship with the experience that we are currently having. That's the only way we can irreversibly change the course of our future.

You suggest that I shouldn't have hope, then?

Once you surrender to the totality of the present moment and, through experience, know that you are not the experience itself, having mental hope is redundant. We don't need to have hope then. We feel and are the hope itself.

You suggest that I shouldn't have dreams?

Either you do something now, or you don't do it now. If a dream is a suggestive narrative about the present moment that doesn't result in any action, but its sole purpose is in the mental activity itself, I suggest that you drop all those dreams – now. A dream is also commonly referred to as an unconscious state we dive into while sleeping over which we have little or no control, and such a state is neither true, necessary nor beneficial. It's more appropriate to swap this absorbed unconsciousness about dreams for a journey-driven intention, a vision, and then to surrender to the joy of not needing to mentally know the result. Once awakened, you will never dream nor sleep again.

You suggest that I shouldn't be optimistic?

Optimism is not the same as forced positivity, or wishful thinking, in order to escape the present experience. Optimism is not denial of the present moment, but rather an experientially knowing that this experience, like all other experiences, will change. Optimism is an inherited quality of embracing the present moment non-judgmentally. I suggest that you feel the optimism and liberation of this statement.

I Am Lost and I Know It All

Most human beings hold on to and carry a set of egoistic identification images that are based on two illusionary core beliefs. In order to live a peaceful and joyful life, we need to let go of these two narratives, and we also need to meet the underlying energetic stream that holds them up, beyond the reactive and judgmental thought itself.

The first belief is our victim story. This is the one in which we are lost, less fortunate, others are to blame, others seem to have it easier, and all bad things seem to always be happening to us. The second belief is our superior story – the one where we know it all, other people are to be conquered, and we ought to aggressively fight our way through life. Since both of these narratives are based on a black-and-white type of thinking, similar to how children with a limited frame of reference operate, we can draw the conclusion that they stem from our childhood. An awakened life is a responsible life, and in order to respond and reclaim our choice, our integrity, we ought to drop all luggage that isn't ours to carry and grow up. This is a personal choice we have, and it is free will by design.

Even if most human beings are navigating primarily by one of these two core beliefs on the visible surface, most alter between the two in different areas of their life experience. It's more accurate to state that we alter between these two states within ourselves and spiral down into a confusion as we continuously try to solve this conflict by projecting it out onto the objects of the world. Our superior narrative may try to fight our sensitive side through outward projections, and our victim narrative projects the same hostile energy toward ourselves. The superior self loves to gossip, and the victimized, sad self loves to talk with others for guidance in order to find some relief from imprinted helplessness. Both are dependent on the external world, and in reality, both are lost.

Ultimately, these are not even our narratives; these are the stories we have absorbed and bought into by watching how our parents, extended family, teachers and those surrounding us navigated life. Since we had no other point of reference, this is the navigation we started out with and may have used so far in our life experience.

However, there's no moment like the present moment to put these inherited stories to rest by not feeding any further energy into phenomena that are neither ours, nor are they at any level considered to be unquestionably true.

So, everything is false?

A narrative is more like a picnic – it's an excursion, but it's not our true home. Most of the things that are given to us by instruction have some truth to them, in a given context and based on a given set of circumstances. If we assign them such meaning and behave in accordance with this wisdom, we are safe. However, most human beings harbor core beliefs based on these narratives and treat them as their home base, and in this context, all narratives should be considered untrue. When I refer to truth, I refer to a phenomenon that under all circumstances is constant and reliable. This is the truth of our true nature, which is the same truth that is contained and unlocked in the present moment.

You mean that I should just let other people push me around?

In this predicament, you are pushing yourself around by acting out narratives that have a root in an internal conflict that isn't even yours in the first place. In order to authentically awaken, and consequently know what our responsibility is in the present moment, we must first put an end to this conflict. This is a gift we give ourselves. The gift is called peace of mind, or more accurately peace *from* mind.

How can you even navigate the world while being this naive?

To be naive is to carry narratives by others and navigate based on other individuals' assumptions with their roots in their childhood experiences. We ought to grow up by finding out the truth for ourselves, and give our once-child self proper and true guidance about life. Being sensitive to our true nature is not the same as being easily hurt or naive. It's about navigating our energy in a manner that truly serves us and the expression we are destined to be in this world. We can't afford to waste our energy on other individuals and their chosen stories if we intend to reach our full potential. We simply need that fuel for our journey home.

But I can feel that other people's behaviorhas an effect on my well-being; should I just let it be?

This is exactly what it is: an effect. Letting it be as it is, and more importantly without outward reaction, will dissolve that effect. An effect is the same as a consequence, and the consequence we feel has a cause in our early behaviors and beliefs around which we have built a false identity. In that sense, it's more accurate to say that other individuals' behaviors touch something unresolved within us. We therefore don't become entangled in conflict and spill further energy into the drama of life by correcting other people as if we were dependent on them. We should instead focus our attention beyond our mental narratives, on our inner body, and feel this energy non-judgmentally in order to dissolve the effects. Once we have surrendered to consistently performing this meditative practice by embracing our Being in the present moment, we get in touch with our higher self. Then the magic starts to occur. This type of drama slowly dissolves and will never, ever have an effect within the field of our awareness again.

Attachment and Reclaiming Your Power of Choice

Human attachment is a mix of survival behavior and imprinting. Understanding how to distinguish these two in the present moment gives us a choice of navigation based on true knowledge that always comes from our own experience. When we can't distinguish the basis of our attachment, we don't know how to navigate life authentically, and that is the root of all kinds of reactive mind patterns via thoughts, emotions and behaviors.

Since human children are utterly vulnerable, we must attach in order to survive. This is a survival instinct that has nothing to do with true love towards the attached objects. We do this instinctively because we love ourselves and this is the game we chose to play in order to get to the next level, where our human vehicle will be mature and developed enough to make a new authentic choice. When we don't reclaim this love for ourselves by consciously making new choices as we progress through life, we get lost in the story of imprinting and reactive behavior. And when we constantly miss this train throughout our adult life, we strengthen the false belief that life is happening "to" us. We lose the only responsibility we actually have, which is the ability to respond to our true self, by getting involved in narratives about others and their choices. We neglect to reclaim what was always ours – our choice.

As we develop throughout life, we receive deeper opportunities to inhabit the full potential of the human form, and if we want to live an awakened and free life, we must make choices based on truth. Ultimately, this assumes that we also need to dismiss what is untrue by not losing ourselves in past imprinting and choices made by others. We are always the ones who will meet the consequences of our choices, even if we act upon other individuals' opinions out of fear. We should therefore realize that we may as well make our own choices consciously and grow from the experience rather than accepting other individuals' concepts as valid and then blaming them for poor output in our life experience.

The first choice we face is that we must consciously, up to the current point of our life experience, reclaim our choices. This is the same as reclaiming our true self. We must respond if we want to be truly free. We must reclaim what was always ours by realizing that we abandoned our true nature, starting in our childhood, in order to survive. As we made this choice, we simultaneously accepted that the cost of this choice was to be imprinted on various levels of our physical, mental, and emotional body. The consequence is that we knowingly accept that this imprinting is unfinished business that we will dissolve at a later stage in our life experience. We will do so when we are fully developed and mature enough to navigate the full potential of our true being. Furthermore, this arrangement is for our benefit, and we chose it out of love – love for ourselves. This is the puzzle of life, and like all puzzles, the result is magnificent once put together. Therefore, we now choose to reclaim our choice by being fully present, responding to our life expression's true purpose and being open to the present moment, no matter what experiences may be manifested.

This game of imprinting also involves us being attached to continuity until we consciously reclaim our choice. Realizing that we are attached to continuity is the same as realizing that we are attached on various levels to our past since we can only try to control a memory that we have already had. This takes us to the next level of insight: we, as the personalized small self, actually fear change because this will disrupt the continuity of what we already know. We are fearful of what may come and how we will take care of ourselves then. Every time we disturb continuity, even if it's a continuity we truly want to disturb, we are embracing an experience of grief. Since we are also collectively imprinted to avoid the experience of grief at all costs, we recognize that authentic change towards becoming our true self will undeniably bring resistance that we ought to overcome. This resistance, which commonly manifests and masks itself as fear in our life experience, is for our own good. This is the key that will unlock our home.

Furthermore, most of the beliefs we currently accept as true are beliefs that we agreed in our childhood were part of a game of imprinting. This is the predicament in which we lost ourselves when we entered what human beings refer to as adulthood. This was never who we truly were, and on a deep level we have always and will always know this to be true. This is also the reason why your true self knows this statement to be true when you read these words. *This is the time we realize that we have never been, could never be, nor ever will be lost.* We have just been lost in a game that we agreed to play in order to survive. No matter how scary and true it may look, it's still a past experience and a game. We agreed to play the game out of love for ourselves. Now is the time for us to realize that we need to adjust our perception on various levels in order to continue the celebration of the game we call life with joy. In this sense, the process of homecoming is not one of learning or doing, but rather a simple process of remembering, knowing and being.

I understand this intellectually and I know what I want, but why is it so uncomfortable to follow through on being true to myself and not listening to others?

This two-sided conflict appears around our definition of responsibility. Firstly, most human beings are imprinted from early childhood with the idea that we are responsible for the quality of other individuals' experiences. This is commonly stated verbally as "You hurt my feelings." This is a fairytale with the intention purely to control and sedate other individuals' behaviors in order to avoid triggers and intensity within our own experience. We simply don't like what we're experiencing, and we outwardly react by asking others to adjust in accordance with our ego's desire.

It's absolutely vital to acknowledge the true meaning behind the word *responsibility*. As you can see from looking at the word, it's a compound of the words *response* and *ability*. The accurate meaning of responsibility is *our ability to respond to ourselves*, and it has absolutely nothing to do with other individuals.

The second part of this conflict is that our past experience is imprinted with situations where we wanted to respond to ourselves but couldn't. We were forced to choose between inhabiting our true self and keeping the attachment to someone in order to survive. This is typically seen in experiences where we needed to listen to our parents, teachers and others in our surroundings as children.

We therefore came to the childish conclusion that responding to ourselves is the same as losing the attachment, and losing the attachment is the same as not surviving. We have a deep subconscious belief that we must choose between being true to ourselves and keeping a relationship. Hence, it can appear immensely threatening on the physical, mental and emotional level to state our truth by responding to ourselves without seeking external approval. On one level, when we start being true to ourselves, the experience may resemble a death experience. This is a natural and healthy evolvement of our being responding to ourselves, and we can let this ancient belief die by feeling it through without seeking external approval.

Furthermore, we realize that we can never be truly abandoned by anyone or anything. On a level of form, we all enter this world in separate bodies and are all equipped with the birthright to be true to ourselves. If our intention is to be true to ourselves, we can't authentically hurt anyone or anything. It undoubtedly can create turbulence in terms of how others place expectations on our form and behaviors, but our sole responsibility is to respond to ourselves by being present. No matter what. We should gently inform others of our true intention and move our attention to our authentic next step. By being honest with ourselves, we are simultaneously being honest with others by giving them the gift of permission to honor their own choices going forward and figure out for themselves what true responsibility is.

Why is it so hard to surrender to the present moment?

When you become aware of being aware, you enter into the true stream of who you truly are. This experience is called being present or being aware of the present moment. This is the same as Being awareness, or consciousness itself. Ultimately, this is who we really are. Being present is exclusively about the being you bring into the present moment, and not about the content you are aware of in the present moment. The content itself consists of the constantly changing objects of life, and in this day and age, we can almost exclusively call it the drama of life. Being present ought not to be confused with forcing an alertness via steering our attention intensively to an object within our field of awareness. While this may give us an experience of aliveness through alertness and to some extent calm the mind, its intention is nevertheless one of doing because we are steering our attention. We ought instead to surrender to the Being of effortlessness in the present moment by simply surrendering to whatever is within our field of awareness, without being attached to or entertaining any particular object or outcome.

The shift into being an awakened being is the shift into awareness of the present moment, which is our true identity, instead of contraction into the never-ending game of changes of the content within the present moment. Contraction into our small personalized self and identification with that experience has a vastly limiting impact on our life experience. When we wrongly believe that we are our experience, we indulge in all sorts of drama, fear and confusion. We simply misuse or ignore our true self.

Certainly, the content of the present moment is also a part of awareness since the experience itself is perceived as real for us, but we are not the experience itself. We unquestionably think and feel what we currently think and feel, but we are not the thinking and feeling. This becomes self-evident when we watch an experience appear in our awareness and then dissolve. You, in your true self, the one who observes your experience, don't dissolve with the thoughts or feelings. You always stay put. That part of you always remains constant, predictable, spacious and reliable. It remains calm, non-judgmental and complete, no matter what experience it encounters. his awareness is who we really are. Awareness is pure, neutral and unpersonal. Nothing can touch it, yet while being aware, we are deeply touched by it.

In my case, the inability to distinguish between these two dimensions created deep suffering and, at its climax, the deep paradox of confusion regarding the belief that I didn't want to die, but I just didn't want to live. What didn't, and couldn't, ever die was what I share with you now: my true self, the pure awareness of that "death" experience. What didn't want to live on, and asked me to observe it dying, was the small, contracted, harshly imprinted personalized self that was full of paradoxes and the root of all my suffering. The clarity to observe these levels within your being gives you great power to navigate your life experience from this point onwards.

Further clarity comes from knowing that *we can't surrender before we know that there's nothing to surrender.* Therefore, we seek clarity until we can embody the experience of surrender. Surrendering is not one big event for which we ought to strive, nor is it a purely mental decision we make. Surrendering is simply an incremental agreement we make with ourselves to be open to embracing everlasting changes, one moment and one breath at a time. Surrendering also demonstrates love for our true being by not adding further conflict to the content of the moment by forcing additional analysis or judgment.

For example, if we observe judgment towards ourselves or others on the level of thought in the present moment, we don't counterstrike by judging the judgment, nor do we make up a new story about what this "means." For our true self, awareness, it never means anything! It's simply another experience.

We therefore simply observe the thought, and we acknowledge that there is a narrative present. We ask ourselves: Where within my inner body, my inner energy field, does this energy resides? We then simply observe it, non-judgmentally and unconditionally. This is what the practice of *being still and knowing that I am God* actually means.

I Have a Moment

We are constantly reminded in our life experience to be still and to know who we really are, by being who we are, although we seldom respond to this call before we hit a personal or collective crisis. We constantly ask each other – Do you have a moment? In the accelerated predicament of distractions that human beings have created collectively, we quite openly say that we don't have a moment. We don't have time. We strive to be busy, which is the same as striving to be unconscious.

Simultaneously, the manufactured thought pattern called time is the only predicament we live in, or escape from. If we want to be free, we must first start to make time. We must consciously embrace the idea – *I have a moment*. We must realize that a moment is all we will ever have. Having a moment is the process of killing the concept of time.

Consciously having a moment, by choosing to acknowledge and therefore love this moment, is a validation that this current moment is the most important moment we will ever have.

This statement can't be overstated. This is the key to liberation: *embracing the present moment by choosing the present moment.* Hence, I suggest that we read the sentence again, slowly, together. Take a couple of deep breaths. Look around at your surroundings in order to anchor yourself in the present moment. Then, read out this statement loudly. Since awareness itself is one, we will all hear you by hearing ourselves reading this statement. This is the relationship we ought to seek with the present moment. This single statement and the conscious quest to live in this manner is the whole meaning of life. This moment is so important, simply because it's all we actually will ever have. Therefore, loving this moment is the same as loving our life.

Living in time is traumatizing for human beings and has consequences on various levels of our life experience. Our true being has no boundaries while form, such as our physical body, has its limitations. It gets tired, and binding it in expectations based on a concept such as time is both traumatizing and unfair treatment of that form. The way out is mental clarity, which we then implement in our life experience as a state of being. We acknowledge the importance and the validity of this moment by consciously choosing to love this moment, no matter what content is presented to us.

I don't have time to meditate and be philosophic about these phenomena. I want to have a life.

Meditation is not some external activity we ought to perform, or an activity to indulge in philosophical subjects about human existence as something outside our everyday life. Meditation is simply being aware of your existence in this moment. The only reason you can have a perception of your existence is the fact that you are aware that you exist. There is only life because you are aware of your life. Therefore, awareness of life is the life itself. In the same way, the moment we stop being aware of our life by checking out of the present moment and into the mental realm of time, that is the exact moment we stop having a life.

I need to work and make a living, and I don't have time to spare on contemplation.

This is an egoistic assumption and a false belief that an awakened life and making a monetary living can't co-exist. We believe the illusion that we must choose one or the other when we in fact can have both on a harmonized level. The truth is that when we are operating from the functional side of our true self, we can *both* be in harmony and make all the money in the world.

This is the fundamental quality of your true self: *oneness*. Most of our false imprinted beliefs are based on duality, which is the same as OR-type thinking. A simple and common example is that we believe we can either have a meaningful family life, *or* a life based on meaningful, intimate friendships and work. In reality, our birthright is that we ought to have both. Duality is the same as conflict since we have two opposites pulling in contradictory directions. This creates friction, which often manifests outwardly as dysfunctional energies of anger or, when pushed inwardly, in blocked states like depression. This spillage of energy results in states of being blocked, and we end up manifesting very little in comparison to our true potential.

We ought to trade this egoistic OR-type thinking for all-inclusive, AND-type thinking. This will unlock untapped energy that we can use to navigate beyond, based on inspiration and enthusiasm. We CAN develop and grow our spiritual life, AND work with something in the present that may not be our purpose further down the road, AND enroll in a course to unfold deeper levels of our creativity, AND start a conscious enterprise, AND be present with our family. This is how we enter the realm of true abundance.

I don't know *if* I'm willing to spend my savings just to be still since such activity doesn't bring me any money.

The question is not whether you can afford to invest in the present moment by living your true purpose, but rather whether you can afford *not* to do so. When we are present and don't live in the manufactured paradigm of time, we *feel* regret instantly. We feel the consequences of our current actions, or non-actions, intuitively. Most human beings refer to this truth of wisdom as our gut feeling. However, to access and unquestionably follow our gut feeling, we must be present. Only in this state are we truly fearless. Furthermore, in the state of presence, a conflict like the one rooted in the statement above can't endure the light of the present moment awareness. We wouldn't be able to tolerate this conflict within the present moment. We would be catapulted into action.

Therefore, it's simplest to point you to the present moment by pointing out the consequence of dwelling in this conflict right here, right now. This is easily accomplished if you think about how your future experience is impacted by not responding to this conflict, right here, right now. This is commonly referred to as pointing you to the experience of regret. If you knew that your physical death was just around the corner, would you happily embrace that state, given how you have prioritized your life journey this far? And remember, you can't bring the energy of money beyond these earthly boundaries.

I hate my work, but I do actually like my personal life better.

As with everything in the universe and therefore in life, we get back what we put in. Most human beings are unquestionably willing to put 80,000 hours or more over their lifespan into something we call our professional life. For many of us, this is typically a fear-driven predicament involving colleagues whom we have not chosen, in which we work on monotonous tasks that someone else has decided for us with little or no creativity. To survive this predicament, we make up all kinds of untrue narratives about responsibilities and adulthood. Furthermore, we attempt to gather a sense of security for later by accumulating money in order to withstand this predicament.

Unfortunately, there's no such thing as a guaranteed "later," and this fearful relationship with the energy of money creates further suffering in our life experience. This dysfunctional relationship with money is very much similar to a substance addiction or a conflict-filled, toxic relationship, where we can't live with them, but we also can't live without them. Once we have the energy of money, we self-sabotage by spending it in a reckless manner, only to find ourselves in the suffering-filled predicament of chasing after more. This strengthens the egoistic beliefs and narratives about other individuals and why we are more, or less, fortunate than they are, which is a waste of the present moment, a waste of the energy of money, and most importantly a waste of the freedom to dwell in harmonization and true abundance with all the energy in the world.

Having a manufactured professional life (the ego) on one hand and a personal life, which is closer to our true self, on the other is living a duality. We ought to consciously choose and integrate the activities we embark upon and be as fully and curiously present as possible while we perform them. By the same token, if we are willing to put so much energy into the predicament of a career, why can't we, over our lifespan, invest at least 20% of those 80,000 hours, or about 16,000 hours of this energy back into a full-time inner journey by accumulating an irreversible, intimate relationship with our true self? Subsequently, we will live one unified life, at peace with all abundance in the world.

I understand all this, but I need to go to work, raise a family and make a living.

The perceived problems and challenges in life are there to support your journey home. Our external life and our internal life are not separate. They are not two discrete entities just because we are imprinted to think, feel and behave in accordance with that illusion. Without challenging relationships, taking care of children, and a noisy work environment, the awakened life is just a theory. No one is asking you to stop your everyday life; the suggestion is simply to be aware and fully present during these activities. You ought to follow your destiny deeply and immensely and to draw deeper wisdom from every experience along the way. We all need you to respond in this manner. We all count on you to navigate in such a way, and this is exactly how important you are to the whole of the universe. We don't need to physically go anywhere in order to unlock heaven on earth. Your true self knows exactly what is required in order for you to reach your highest potential. Your task is simply to be still, listen and follow.

Beyond Anxiety and Panic Attacks

Anxiety is a state that is broadly used by the mental body when the inner body's fear resonance arises, the root of which we can't explain in the circumstances of our present moment. This typically occurs when our inner charged body raises the intensity of the experience in the present moment in a way we can't mentally explain, and we then run into the experience of anxiety. In this sense, the easiest way to name the energy state of anxiety is to call it unexplainable fear. This also implies that, once consciously uncovered or explained by the wisdom of our own experience, all anxiety will disappear from our life experience. Firstly, if we are going to transform into the totality of eternal peace and joy, we can't afford to have different energy states being named by others that we simply absorb as true and then act accordingly by enforcing these beliefs in our own experience. If we want to transform the experience of anxiety, we ought to take responsibility and find out, in our own experience, what anxiety is. Anxiety ought to be treated as a concept that explains a certain state we experience until we discover what this state means and, based on this wisdom, transcend it.

We are not born as anxious beings; all of us have memories of being present, curious, and fully alive at least at some point in our life. We ought therefore to point our being to this experience of total fulfillment as not only a possible and permanent state, but as our birthright. What anxiety existed in this state before someone taught us that we are anxious and we bought into that story? Being anxious is an experience we have and not an identification of or a statement about who we really are. We move beyond anxiety by changing our relationship with this energetic state and gently moving from *this is terrifying* to *this is interesting*.

I can mentally understand this, but I still feel overwhelmed by my anxiety.

Being able to state that you are overwhelmed is already the first stage of disidentification with the concept of anxiety. The next stage is to identify on what level of your being this overwhelm occurs and then to keep observing deeper layers of your experience.

My thoughts are overwhelming me; they just keep spinning around what I should be doing.

This is typically self-inflicted anxiety by identification with the patterns of thought. We mentally reject the present moment and want to escape to a thought's ideas of the future. This creates an inner conflict between where we physically are and where we mentally "should" be, in turn escalating an emotional, claustrophobic fear response. This spirals us into a vicious circle of conflicted energy on different levels of our being that we call anxiety. Anxiety ends when the conflict ends. Since this particular conflict occurs when we don't accept our life as valid and honor our life journey, in order to put this conflict and the anxiety to rest, we ought to use our free will, our choice, and choose this moment, and therefore our life, intentionally.

Yes, but sometimes it's not my pattern of thoughts; the anxiety or fear just comes over me.

Our charged inner body keeps the score of all unfinished clusters of physical sensations and emotions on a cellular level.

These clusters can be activated within our awareness both unconsciously and consciously. When we are unconscious, we call them our triggers, and when we act on them, they drive our reactive behaviors since we are unwilling to put our awareness on our inner body and be present. Even if we don't consciously admit it, we feel afraid of our subconscious mind, or our unfinished energetic past within us. This manifests as an underlying sense of unsafety within our life experience, which we typically box in and label generalized anxiety. We can at any point start dissolving these energies by striving to be present and put awareness on our inner body. To put an end to this conflict, and anxiety, we ought to use compassion towards ourselves and embrace the wisdom of our inner body experience consciously.

Is this the same with panic attacks?

When we have an intense perception of an inner experience that we can't mentally explain within the circumstances of our present moment, we get disorientated. This disorientation instinctively activates, on a primitive level, a response of fight, flight or freeze. The foundation of a panic attack is when we enter the uncomfortableness of the "freeze" realm. When the inner body energy reaches a certain level, we don't have the ability to fight or to flee, and we then add a thought to the cocktail, we typically run into an experience that we call a panic attack.

Animals don't experience this; they remain present in their inner body experience and embrace this inner energy state in the present moment. If you have ever watched a dog's reaction to fireworks on New Year's Eve, you may have noticed how the dog shakes vigorously when experiencing fear that stems from the fact that he can't visually place from where the danger originates. When he doesn't know where to run, or what to attack, his last option is to freeze. Since he has accumulated an immense amount of energy to fight or flee, he needs to burn this energy off in the "freeze" state in order to remain present and healthy. This is where the magic happens. The dog doesn't transform this energy into negative mental narratives about his self-image, nor does he schedule a shrink appointment – he simply starts to *shake this energy off*.

On this level, we ought to learn from the dog and ask our body to move and shake until the energy is in balance. It's neither necessary nor beneficial to stir up our inner experience to the turbulent level of panic attacks consciously. This typically drives our mental narratives in a negative manner and burns an immense amount of energy with little resulting wisdom. Even if a panic attack is a healthy reaction to what our body-mind perceives as danger, and we ought to be thankful for and in awe of these mechanics, it's not a necessary state to strive for when observing our experience. It's much more beneficial to meet this "freeze" energy on lower energetic levels where we can consciously, while anchored in the present moment, put our attention on them and observe them one breath at a time.

Beyond Addictive Behaviors

All addictions are an unconscious search for enlightenment. In the beginning, while still potent, they give us temporary relief, or a sample of our true Being. Addictions are also unconscious behaviors we indulge in when we can't contain the present moment as it is on various levels of our being. This is the toolset of behaviors and substances we use to navigate life to the best of our ability until we gather sufficient consciousness to dissolve this paradigm and live in our Being organically. The addictive behaviors are entertained out of love for our true self, even if on the surface they come across as highly dysfunctional. The love thrives on the willingness to dissolve the ego and be fully present, even if it's with the assistance of this set of behaviors and substances. The dysfunction thrives on the fact that a part of these behaviors is unconscious and therefore both unpredictable and uncontrollable since they are rooted in fear, or escape from the present moment. Since one of the universe's fundamentals is the law of cause and effect, what starts with suffering will eventually end in suffering. Even if these behaviors give us a temporary sense of safety and control, the endgame always carries the consequence of the kick-off.

The greatest consequence of entertaining addictive behaviors is unconsciousness from the present moment, where our ability to be consciously connected to our Being is at various levels shut off. This results in inconsistent, raw, and instinctive navigation based on our unconscious patterns, which means that the cost of addictive assistance is giving up a part of our integrity.

Driving our vehicle in this disordered manner results in various self-inflicted accidents, which can all be categorized under the umbrella of drama, guilt, shame, and regret. All of these energetic states are just indications that we should stop the vehicle, be still, and gather new wisdom on how to authentically operate our being.

Furthermore, we are socially and culturally imprinted on various levels to praise certain addictive behaviors as "successful" while others are despised as "unsuccessful" in the eyes of our peer groups and society. This dysfunction further feeds the increased separation within the addicted individuals and results in illusionary narratives based on collective shame.

Therefore, we can only move beyond addictions by recognizing these mechanics, remembering that we are all *born innocent*, and making a conscious intention to find the truth about our true nature in our experience. This will manifest the external circumstances needed for us to transform beyond the addictive predicament.

This is a fairly easy way to see all addictive behaviors as the same.

I am just pointing to the simple mechanics of our Being: once we understand the mechanics in our own experience, they are all the same. On the level of form, they may have different short- and long-term consequences that may or may not be visible, but the core, beyond human-constructed narratives, is always the same. Most human beings carry a dreadful addiction to thinking, which we accept as normal, even if it has tremendous consequences on our suffering, behaviors and environment. Furthermore, a vast majority of human societies accept the recreational use of alcohol, a predicament that has a tremendous consequence on our collective well-being. With this said, there's no rational logic to building and identifying with any human-constructed story on the level of different addictive behaviors. You can simply see it, as it is but not worse than that, surrender to it, and then take the necessary action to move beyond this predicament. This is the start of the journey home to your true self.

I don't understand how I can promise myself I'll stop a habit, but then suddenly let myself down and do it again.

The unconscious behavior based on resistance to an underlying energetic state that drives your habitual actions is not conscious to your mental body. Subsequently, this confusion and paradox arises between the conscious decision and the unconscious behaviors. It's commonly called a blind spot until you put the honest and non-judgmental light of awareness on it.

Only you can do this for yourself. We can, by enforcing mental discipline, consciously stop different habitual behaviors, but as long as we are still suppressing our subconscious mind in the present moment, the addictive behaviors will show up in other forms in our life experience. We don't dissolve these patterns and energy through this approach; we merely postpone the energy or move it to another dimension. This route of navigation further drives confusion because we then don't mentally understand why it appears again. It appears simply because we're refusing to non-judgmentally embrace it and feel it. Understanding the mechanics of your being by maintaining a firm commitment and willingness to find your true self, no matter what, will set you free. Addictive behaviors are the hardest way of trying to live an easy life.

Others says it's my bad character or lack of discipline that makes me unable to stop these dysfunctional habits.

This is a human-constructed belief that needs to be examined in your own experience and itself has a root in an addiction – *dependence on others' approval*. Absorbing collective low-level energies in the form of thought patterns and then behaving as if these are true is limiting us from moving beyond the current predicament. We ought to redirect our energy, to move on, by setting an intention to find other individuals with higher consciousness within this area who will point us to the truth. On the dysfunctional side of all addictions is suffering and confusion. On the bright side, fully surrendering to your powerlessness over your addictive behaviors and then moving beyond through a sincere intention to put an end to this suffering is the finest catalyst to enlightenment. There's no authentic power or predictability in the false self. In the true self, there's all the power and continuity of the world.

I am addicted to training and exercise, but that's hardly bad for you, right?

Various addictive behaviors will have various consequences on the level of your physical form, although the important question here is whether you can afford to be dependent on the illusion that you are your body. Being dependent on physical abilities as the primary way of navigating the purpose and wisdom in one's life is both limiting and a fragile way of being. With every breath we take, we age, and the physical form changes its boundaries. Going beyond the level of physical form will make training truly enjoyable, in contrast to the forceful "project managing" of one's energetic states.

Beyond Diagnosis and Chronic Illness

Just like all human-constructed concepts that aim to describe an experiential state, a diagnosis is a mental description of a pattern under a set of circumstances. A diagnosis is characteristically only valid as long as the pattern meets a set of parameters and a particular frequency level. Since most of our diagnoses are subject to subjective input by someone with experience, the responsibility for a diagnosis is shared between the one asking for and the one giving the diagnosis.

Whenever we ask for an examination, we intentionally agree to receive a conceptual and mental description of a human experience. We must therefore recognize that we have an essential role in any diagnosis that we may get. This includes our consent to share our experience with another individual, the interpretation that individual makes based on their own experience, and most importantly the meaning we assign to this diagnostic experience. All diagnoses start with a hypothesis and can only operate within the boundaries of what's currently known to mankind. Furthermore, societal and cultural structures that operate within our predicament have a different level of consciousness and ability to point us to the truth of our experience and therefore various abilities to alleviate our suffering and pain. We ought to remain curious and embrace our true nature by searching for the truth, beyond our predicament. We ought not to identify with any experience by indulging in further self-inflicted pain and strengthening attachment to our diagnosis.

You mean that my diagnosis is untrue, then?

I'm pointing out that diagnoses are true on one level, within the boundaries and the contexts within which they operate. If we alter our perception and take a higher stand in our true self, the context and our perception will change. This applies especially to the meaning we assign to our experiences, or in this context, our diagnoses. When the level of our consciousness transforms, our experiences will transform, and when our experiences transform, so do our relationships with our diagnoses.

This is easy to state, but I have chronic conditions.

Human beings use the word "chronic" to describe an experience whenever we can't label and explain an experience within the limitations of time. It's more accurate and displays more integrity to state that we *don't know* when we examine the personal or collective unknown. In that sense, all of life is always chronic since the physical sensations and experiences are constantly changing. However, someone else, outside your predicament or with higher level consciousness in this area, may know more or may have the keys that will set you free.

So, what do you suggest I do?

I always suggest that you firstly be. Allow the state to be as it is, non-judgmentally, in the present moment. Put your awareness on your inner body and embrace your whole Being. This is the same as demonstrating love for your true nature. This may not immediately alleviate your physical pain or restore your energy, but it will end your suffering. Once your suffering ends, you will be able to authentically communicate with your higher self and take appropriate actions based on truth. This will transform your life experience, and the consequence will be peace.

You suggest that I just sit down, dying, and wait for some sort of miracle?

I am not suggesting passivity; I am suggesting action from stillness – appropriate action from peace, and not fear. I am also suggesting that you allow that illusion in you, which is afraid of death, to die. Then you will experience rebirth to peace. This is the miracle. Ask for it – they happen all the time.

PART II

KNOWING YOURSELF

Movement beyond feeling

"What you feel is what you feel, but it's not who you are."

Beyond Existential Anxiety

Not knowing through experience who we really are and why we are here creates at best a predicament of underlying lifelong low-level anxiety. Some of us are more acutely aware of this fact than others, although, sooner or later, no one can escape it. Since most of us, at least in the modern world, distract ourselves from this truth by being busy, we consider this type of behavior to be normal. But then when we get still, and alone, we meet this truth face to face. We feel deep inside that something is not right with how we navigate life. Typically, we can't say what's wrong, but at our core we feel that something is not right.

We move beyond this predicament by setting an intention to answer two vital questions. Once these two questions are answered within our own experience, everything will be answered. In that sense, there's only one purpose to our life, and that is to answer these questions on all levels of our being, and then to recognize them to be true in our life experience. The questions are:

1. Who am I?
2. What is the meaning and purpose of my being here?

In truth, it's only necessary to answer one question – "Who am I?" The second question, and all other questions in life, will automatically be answered after the first. However, since most of us are stuck and confused by searching for meaning in what we physically do, it's beneficial to point our being to both questions since they will drive movement in our search. All human beings are searching for the answer and resolution to these questions, even if most of humankind does it both unconsciously, based on an imprinted false self, and in reverse order. This paradox is the root of all our suffering, fears, and separation.

All human beings are forced to face these questions at some point, even if we don't respond to them consciously. The tragedy is meeting them in panic just before our physical death. The amount of content we produce with testimonies from the elderly about what they wish they had done earlier in life and our obsession with bucket lists is evidence enough that most of us live unconsciously. We don't actually live; it's more accurate to describe our existence as barely existing in a continuous state of regret. The time is never right – the time is only right – right now. The only way to put this paradox to rest is to awaken to a total transformation, home to our true self – the one we were meant to be and the one that is in alignment with our true calling. This simple quest will liberate us all.

What do you mean when you say the questions should be answered on all levels of my being?

Firstly, we ought to search until we are consistent on the physical, mental and emotional level about the true knowing of who we are. We ought to search until we can contain the present moment non-judgmentally – just as it is. You may have a mental image of who you think you are and may be able to contain it as long as your physical body is in lighter energies or not aching. But when there is a disturbance, or rather a greater intensity in the present moment on one level, are you able to contain the same truth, or do you relapse into unconscious behaviors? When we do that, we acknowledge that we're still thinking and acting on a level as if we were our physical bodies; then we can get back into the stillness and surrender to what is. Simultaneously, when we lose ourselves in a thought pattern, we move our attention to the present moment by consciously connecting our breathing and putting our awareness on our inner body. All of these are natural techniques to restore harmony, to be safe, or to go home. If you find one, you find all.

I have felt my whole life that that there's something wrong with me. Is this the reason?

When we question the core belief, or the illusion, of who we are, our imprinting tends to counterstrike immediately by giving us a mind state of collective shame. Some feel this separation, or imprinting injection, acutely in their childhood as a deep sense of separation from their family and of not being understood. This is because as children, we are told on various levels who we are before we ourselves develop the capacity to ask the question. We get a name that we didn't choose; others choose the clothes we wear; most of our friends tend to be chosen for geographical and logistical reasons rather than energetic fit. Children are more or less trapped in a predicament until they have sufficient size and form to navigate on their own. Most of our egoistic self is based on these previously absorbed beliefs, and our responsibility as adults is to put awareness on this predicament and reclaim our choice. Beliefs are imprinted by a certain set of repetitive observations and actions and are similarly dismantled by a certain set of repetitive observations and actions, or rather non-actions.

You talk often about illusions and now you say that we need repetition or unlearning. If it's an illusion, why do we need to repeat it?

It takes a large amount of energy to imprint an illusion, but to unwrap one is effortless. We simply put our awareness on the mechanics behind it, and immediately we see it to be untrue. There's nothing more to understand about the mechanics of the trick once you know that it's a trick. When I talk about repetition, it's solely about a non-doing, about being still in situations when former imprinting, or the illusion, asks us to act as if it were true. The repetition is not to fall for the trick; neither is it to repeat the imprinted need of trying to mentally understand the trick again (and again). Instead, we move to the next level with grace – we *feel* our inner body non-judgmentally.

The Charge of Anger and Your "Life Story"

Most of our negative and distorted mental thought patterns have their root in unfinished energetic patterns in our past experiences. All of this accumulated, energetically unfinished business creates an inner body charge that we don't know how to cope with or diffuse in the present moment. On the level of thought, this charge drives our present experience and generates narratives in a judgmental, hostile, and self-negative manner. Since the charged energies have their roots in many different past experiences, the thought patterns are both conflicting and constantly creating inner body friction within the field of our awareness. The charge of anger also drives us to immobility, or fear, since we are afraid of getting in touch with this energy. We are simply afraid of our accumulated anger. The consequence of carrying this inner body charge, the narratives, and the conclusions we draw from this uncomfortable experience is manifestation of states such as anxiety, depression, despair, and panic attacks.

One practice to move beyond these blockages is to consciously embrace our fear, anger, and grief by consciously embracing our "life story." This is a way of helping our mental body to release the underlying energies within our inner body in a seemingly structured manner. Otherwise, we are at risk of staying blocked, stuck in the mental realm where we typically indulge in physical behaviors like attending never-ending verbal therapy sessions. The sole purpose of any verbal encounter ought to be to point us toward an energetic inner body experience. Once the inner body charge is felt non-judgmentally, all narratives dissolve.

Hence, the only authentic intention with structuring and writing out our life story ought to be to access the inner body charge. Once we are fearlessly in touch with our inner body, we ought to let go of our life story. Many find it beneficial to manifest this letting go of the life story via a physical activity, such as burning what they have written in a bonfire.

I'm confused; you say we should let go of all narratives, but you're simultaneously suggesting that we embrace our "life story"?

Before we can enter, redecorate, and live compassionately in our own home, which is to a large extent our inner body, we must clear the room of everything that isn't ours. In order to know what's truly ours and what's borrowed, it's useful to take an inventory. Before we can truly let go, we must know what we are letting go of. We can't surrender if we think, act or believe our narratives to be totally true or believe that they serve us. For most human beings, at least in the modern world, we are so stuck in our mental narratives that we may feel the need to consciously go through, preferably in writing, our mental life story.

When we embrace the story, and more importantly feel through the underlying energetic emotions in every belief statement, the fragmented story dissolves on the level of thought patterns. If you ask Being, you will be shown whether this is a necessary or authentic part of your journey for the unfolding of your soul's desire.

What should I do with my "life story," then?

A calm mental body is a sorted mental body, and a sorted mental body is consciously investigated terrain. This is not a practice of digging into our past; it's a practice whereby we invite our past into the present. We simple uncover beliefs that have a real impact on our current life experience. Since the ego survives solely on our unconsciousness, it can't survive such an honest inventory in the present moment. Note that we ought to consciously embrace our life story, which indicates that we ought to examine the effects on various levels of our being, including the level of the inner body. We ought to feel the consequences of this hostile charge of anger on the inner body level in order to know, and therefore dissolve, this story by feeling it through. Once you commit to this process, you will be gently moved from negative narratives to more heroic ones. Then it's time to truly let go of all stories and dwell in your pure Being – *by the grace of forgiveness.*

Forgiveness and True Revenge

Human beings have an imprinted and distorted concept of what forgiveness is, and an important part of the journey to peace and joy is the ability to calibrate our understanding of forgiveness. Firstly, human beings are imprinted, on various levels of our being, to believe that forgiving others who have acted unjustly is equal to justifying the act that has been done "to" us. This offended self, sometimes called the little self, or the ego, is trying to find balance by holding on to grudges and seeking revenge. This is always performed on the mental plane and in the constructed concept of time.

We are further imprinted to believe that forgiveness has to do with other individuals through early instructions to ask others to "forgive us" for something we have learned to feel guilty or shamed about. To add further confusion, it's not uncommon for children to be forced to ask for forgiveness even if others committed the injustice to start with. This confused us and trapped us in blocked energies of anger.

None of these concepts are ours to carry as adults, and we ought to calibrate this perception matrix by first adjusting our concept of forgiveness. We do so by realizing that *forgiveness is a gift we give ourselves by not entering into conflict with the present moment*. We forgive by allowing the present moment to be as it is, and by trusting that the universal law of cause and effect will always even everything out. By and large, we are all walking the same path, and no one can truly escape the consequences of their actions even if it can periodically appear that way on the surface. We may successfully distract ourselves for periods of time, but sooner or later we will all face this universal truth.

Furthermore, we must realize that others are not so much doing anything to us as they are doing it to themselves by acting from the ego, or small self. The consequence of this behavior within their life experience is more than enough. No one can escape this truth if we broaden our perspective. Lastly, we must stop asking others to do for us things which are our responsibility to do. Therefore, we stop asking others to "forgive us." We move beyond this predicament by forgiving ourselves for believing this limiting belief by adjusting it in accordance with our new understanding within our own experience.

At this stage we can differentiate forgiveness from reconciliation. To forgive, we don't need anything or anyone since it's a pure internal agreement based on the wisdom of our experience that neither we nor others are our set of imprinted behaviors. No one is to blame for unconscious behavior simply because we don't want to entertain internal conflicts that the present moment ought to be different than it is in some way. Most of us know that we will sooner or later forgive someone or something by accepting all situations as they are. If we already know this, why not drop the resistance and forgive now? Nothing changes from having a mental image that a certain amount of "time" needs to elapse in order for us to find a situation acceptable. This is self-inflicted suffering and can only result in a future present moment of regret. Therefore, we forgive *everything* in order to feel peace right now. When we have made an authentic decision to forgive, we will notice a deep insight into our life experience that will manifest as an irreversible state of peace. This undoubtable experiential wisdom demonstrates that when we forgive others, we are in reality forgiving ourselves. This can only be experienced once we choose to move beyond our mental narratives around forgiveness and the involved individuals, places and circumstances.

Furthermore, we ought to authentically feel our inner body energy, which we earlier referred to as "anger," after we have made a conscious decision to forgive and dismiss the individual, place or circumstance as responsible for this energy. For most of us, this shift may take some practice since we are habitually trained to blame. In the memory recall, we may feel a deep stickiness between the inner body charge and the mental circumstances, resulting in an intensive present moment state. We should observe this play and aim to maintain our focus and attend to our inner body sensations through conscious breathing. Incrementally, as the charge dissolves, the narratives dissolve. Then the previously blocked energy is free and un-personal. It's not connected to any narrative and can freely flow through us and liberate us. We are no longer stuck in blockages of blame by patterns of jealousy or envy. This freed up energy is now carrying us into action and alignment with our true purpose, and we are thankful for this gift of forgiveness.

However, for reconciliation to occur, we need a common and conscious consent on our part and on the part of the other individual. This is where we often agree to do our utmost to recognize our current unconsciousness and commit to an undertaking of responding lovingly, rather than reacting with hostility, in present moments to come. Reconciliation is also a gift we give ourselves. It's a gift of choice to remove energy from individuals, places, or circumstances that are not yet able or willing to respond consciously to this quest. It's also a gift of continuity, to grow with those who are ready to take responsibility. We must always surrender to the process of forgiveness before we include other individuals in the process of reconciliation. We ought always to forgive first in order to achieve balance within our own experience before engaging in any behavior. Then, based on the wisdom of forgiveness, we will intuitively know if we ought to embark on the journey of reconciliation and how that set of actions, or non-actions, may manifest.

How will I know if I've done something wrong?

Our true self, no matter what our individual form has done, can't be wrong or broken. This doesn't mean that we don't take responsibility for our unconscious behaviors caused by our imprinting. It simply means that we all are created perfectly and we all deserve to be treated that way. Usually, human be-ings use the phrase "I'm sorry" to bring balance to the pres-ent moment if they feel they have authentically trespassed against another's integrity. That's a suggestion. When you are present, you are in accordance with your Being's desire. You will then know what's true, what's not, and what action is ap-propriate to take (or, more often, not to take) in order to bring justice to the present moment. Since our Being is always in perfect harmony, you are always in perfect harmony when in touch with it. You true self can't have any human-constructed concepts such as guilt or shame since it was created perfectly. These concepts are better described as small energy fields that help you navigate the energetic balance within the present moment. Further entertaining any mental concepts is neither necessary nor beneficial.

So, you suggest that I just forgive everything and always reconcile with others?

I suggest that you embark on the process of forgiveness and reconciliation in order to gather wisdom on what truly unites us all – beyond all the imprinted fairytales of the world. Forgiving is for giving yourself *peace from mind* by allowing the present moment to be as it is, without interference. We forgive because we love our true self. It's all an action of love for yourself, and thus we ought to take all necessary steps until we know this to be true in our life experience. We then reconcile because we recognize that we are all perfect on the level of our Being. Reconciliation is also an act of service and doesn't mean that we have to become best friends with individuals who may keep hurting us with their unconscious behavior. Once you have authentically forgiven, you will know that forgiveness and reconciliation actually occur simultaneously in the present moment. They are not two separate entities. The gift of forgiveness is an endless breeze of unconditional love. Once we have truly experienced that everything is perfect, just as it is, we don't need the concept of forgiveness nor of reconciliation; we will simply be here, *for giving*.

What should I do with all this angry energy and deep sense of need for revenge that is left on the inner body level?

The personalized, little self, or the ego, is always afraid and seeks revenge in both a directly visible and a non-holistic manner. When operating solely from this small, personalized dimension, we feel a deep sense of aloneness, helplessness, and vulnerability. This is simply the mechanics and limitations of localizing something eternal like awareness into a form. Attempting to navigate solely from this dimension creates disease and friction in our life experience. It's an illusion that we are alone, although the illusion appears to be real since at this level we simultaneously think, feel and behave as if we were our thoughts, feelings and physical body. There's nothing more to understand nor be frustrated about at this level. This is a simple fact about how different levels of our being operate. An intelligent being understands this play from experience and navigates in accordance with what is true and appropriate.

You can always help the ego to dissolve itself by pointing it to true revenge. That is, there is only one form of revenge that will solve all injustice. This revenge is to put all the previous conflicted energy into finding, knowing and then being your true purpose. When this is accomplished – all is accomplished. Then the small, personalized self, or the ego, will never bother you again; the two of you will become one, and together live a happy life for an eternity. First forever and then always.

From Acceptance to Allowance

Human beings are usually pointed to an experience of peace via a signpost word – *acceptance*. Acceptance is an experience whereby we surrender to the physical, mental or emotional circumstances of the present moment. Acceptance is lack of resistance. Acceptance is flow. Acceptance is also typically considered to be a premature mental state that occurs before we can truly let go of the conflicted inner body state. Nevertheless, most human beings are imprinted that we ought to do something, usually run a mental process, before we consider a situation acceptable or not. Unfortunately, this process more often than not strengthens the mental body, and the ego, by inflicting new judgment on the level of thought upon a situation that in itself is always neutral. This has a consequence on our ability to non-judgmentally embrace the present moment since we are interfering with a new self-made character that neutralizes the first act of acceptance.

Therefore, in order to take the direct path to resolving any conflict within the present moment, we ought to move from acceptance to *allowance*. For most of us, allowance is closer to a neutral state of non-action. Allowance is also closer to the act of humility, which is the same as surrendering to the process of not knowing – or to the joy of the unknown.

Does this really matter? I mean, it's just semantics, right?

When you read this statement, it may feel obvious for your mental body and it may seem to all be just semantics, but this assumption needs to be truly examined in your life experience in order for you to know how profound this change in perception might be. When the intensity in the present moment is high-pitched, this single movement through a word, accompanied by deeper energetic states, will make all the difference in the world regarding how fast we can anchor back in the love of the present moment.

I am judgmental sometimes, and I really try to accept things and stop being judgmental.

By allowing the first judgmental thought to be, we dissolve and put the whole game to rest. By creating an "accepting" thought as a strategy to fight and argue with the initial judgmental thought, we simply add fuel to the fire. We now have a new judgmental thought that we call an experience of "acceptance" that judges the initial judgmental thought. That thought was originally just neutral energy appearing within our field of awareness. We put this game to rest by allowing any thoughts to be and dissolve without acting or behaving like any of their content is personal.

I always thought that I should accept myself; why is that wrong?

The human-constructed concept of acceptance has its roots in the human-created and primarily accepted concepts of guilt and shame. Then we create a new concept that aspires to give us some relief from this highly conditional state of mental suffering, which we call accepting ourselves and which is basically a sneak peek of who we really are. This is typically referred to as ignorance in various ancient teachings because in doing this, we ignore, or miss the point, of our true self.

We truly accept ourselves by allowing ourselves to be ourselves. Allowing our whole being to be, just as it is, is the same as demonstrating love for ourselves.

But isn't allowance also just a concept?

In this context, allowance ought to be treated as a signpost to settle the conflict of resistance within and toward our life experience as it unfolds in the present moment. *Our level of resistance to the present moment represents the amount of compassionate allowance we require.* Once resistance dissolves, so does the concept of allowance. We are then simply ourselves. And yes, it is a concept – until we allow the allowance to be. Can we, for now, demonstrate allowance by allowing the statement of allowance to be?

Novelty Brings Change
and Change Brings Resolution

In order for anything to change, or dissolve, its original pattern needs to be disturbed. A pattern is simply a predictive chain of events under a set of circumstances. In the context of this work, when we refer to a pattern, we mean a pattern or a cluster of physical sensations, thoughts, and emotions. Even if we are behaving as if we are a mystery to ourselves, most of our behaviors in the external world are simply a set of past memories that raises the intensity in our present moment to a certain level until we act and escape into unconscious actions. Since our being is interconnected, the various levels both drive and feed each other.

For example, identifying with a given pattern of thoughts in the present moment may drive a mental image, a memory, that creates a physical sensation in the chest area, and thereafter an emotional reaction of crying. We can call this experience a cluster of grief. If we were to continuously let this experience flow through us, we would always be present, joyful, and fully alive. Unfortunately, collectively, human beings don't navigate our lives in this organic manner. We have created a suffering predicament that we call time wherein we must develop the art of suppression in order to live in that mental place. This predicament of constantly aborting the natural flow of our being creates fragments and accumulates clusters of incomplete physical sensations, thoughts and emotions. When we get still, or aim to be present, these accumulated and unfinished clusters of physical sensations, thoughts and emotions float up into our awareness in order to be validated as true at some point in our past experience. We validate them and let them run their course to completion by demonstrating love for our true self – which is the same as accepting them, which is the same as allowing them, which is the same as non-judgmentally observing and feeling them through.

I understand this in theory, but I don't have time to follow through with every sensation or memory that comes up.

This is an imprinted egoistic assumption that we must do something in addition to whatever is already happening. I am suggesting quite the opposite: simply putting attention on our awareness non-judgmentally and allowing what's already occurring beneath the surface to be recognized as valid – to surrender to the present moment unconditionally. If we want to experience heaven on earth, we must be willing to embrace our whole being organically, now.

This is tremendously uncomfortable; I'm afraid of facing this content.

For the vast majority of human beings, this experience is uncomfortable since we have suppressed a large amount of content and have been simultaneously imprinted to resist and fight this healthy experience of regulation. However, while pain may be the reason we change, uncomfortableness is the reason we grow. We are built to regain balance on all levels of our being by not interfering with human-constructed narratives about experiences.

Many modern diagnoses around mental health involve labeling these originally healthy experiences with different names, or even going so far as to call them our "demons." It's more accurate to call them our "children" from the past, who are coming home to us in the present moment to get a hug. We ought to give them an unlimited number of hugs by embracing the validity of the present moment. Nothing's wrong; we are here, now, and fully alive.

How would I even function in the real world if I implement this strategy of going into different patterns?

Changing a pattern doesn't mean that we need to go into the content of the pattern in order for resolution to occur. It's quite the opposite. Trying to bring clarity to a pattern by adjusting the narrative of the pattern itself may give us some initial relief, but we are still enforcing the belief that the pattern is true. We are left on the level of the pattern. If we wish to truly transform the quality of our life experience, our intention must be to transcend the pattern. A pattern changes at its core once we take a higher stand in our focus, when we observe it as deeply and intimately as we are able to. An inner transformation is exclusively about observation, or awareness of the content in the present moment. It's never about the content itself.

Inner Body Charge
– Contraction and Expansion

Once we have settled our conflicting energies by consciously forgiving, and then discarded the narratives around our life story to the point where we don't intentionally enforce mental images from the past onto the present moment, we then move deeper into our inner body. One fundamental dimension that can't be emphasized enough is the power of forgiveness. This is an absolutely vital step in moving beyond before we can live comfortably in our inner body. We can't afford to have mental confusion and hostile revenge energy if we wish to live comfortably and peacefully in our home. Our inner body is our home and, together with our breath, the most direct path to present moment awareness. *The ability to stay anchored in the present moment is in direct proportion to our ability to be connected non-judgmentally to our inner body.* The deeper we get into our inner body, the more aware we become about the different states floating in and out of our field of awareness. We go into states, or waves, of contraction and expansion.

This is the stage in which we have dis-identified with our mental body, our narratives, and we are willing to be, non-judgmentally, within our inner body. Once we commit to this compassionate quest, our inner body responds by opening up energies that have been blocked. We move into what we may refer to as states of contraction and expansion. This paradigm is very different from the previous mental body state in which we alternated between fear and hope, or past and future, in the sense that contraction and expansion experiences are encountered in the present moment. Awareness is here now.

At this stage, we have also lovingly left behind the mental necessity to understand and name experiences before agreeing to feel through them non-judgmentally by putting awareness on our inner body. The deeper in we go, the less ability and inclination we experience to name our feelings. We neither know nor need to know the root cause of this energy. It may have its roots in an experience before we developed our ability to talk, or it may be a collective energetic charge. It may be energy from the moment of our birth. Since our collective energy is non-personal, it's neither necessary nor beneficial to search after a mental answer. We trust that if a mental answer is necessary for our development, it will be revealed in the present moment.

The contraction state is best described as a state of localized awareness, and for the vast majority of human beings this experience is initially considered to be uncomfortable. The contraction state is a multi-dimensional experience of past mental images, physical sensations and emotional states that have nothing to do with the present moment. The key words when going into the contraction state are simply mental confusion and fear. This state is also recognized by an overall sensation within our experience of unsafety, entrapment and generalized hopelessness. The way out is by going in – into the inner body. We simply place our awareness on our breath until the awareness of our inner body is restored. This is the same as stating that we put our awareness on our inner body and feel the intensity of the experience until the present moment is restored.

Deactivation of a contraction state is typically an energy completion, such as a crying response, sensations of being cold or shaking of the body. All of these are natural and healthy states of past energetic completion and a natural part of an awakening to your true self. Our true self dwells just beneath these energetic states. The less resistance we enforce on our experience, the sooner the contraction state will be integrated into our life experience. This experience is also widely known in various teachings as the death of the ego or the dark night of the soul. The key phrase is *surrender by allowance*. We trust our nervous system; we trust that we are built to survive, and we know that the worst has already happened since we have already experienced the actual situation in the past. We are now simply embracing the energetic leftovers. Surrender to the present moment and feel the power of your inner body's ability to restore harmony.

Although the contraction state may be uncomfortable, it offers a tremendous gift once we first non-judgmentally allow it, and later compassionately embrace it. It catapults us into the expansion state of wisdom. This is the gift we receive for non-judgmentally embracing what we may observe as the storm. Expansion is also the state in which we may perceive the sun to be shining again, and we are reborn and safe. We intuitively gain access to the wisdom and the necessity of this experience. We grow.

This has been going on for a while within my life experience; how long will it last?

This process is unfolding at the pace that is most beneficial for your soul and for the whole. We ought not to rush or push any experience, but rather simply do our utmost to be there, as the observer of the experience. The process will deepen your wisdom of who you are and give you the gift of absolute knowing, through experience, that you are not your experience.

When this is completed, we will gradually move beyond the states of contraction and expansion. The body knows its own way home, and that journey itself is timeless at any given moment. We don't interrupt that process with unnecessary imprinted drama by putting conceptual timeframes and expectations in place. The body needs to go through what it needs to go through in order for harmony to occur. We assist this process by demonstrating love for ourselves, which is the same as being unconditional and non-judgmental towards this process at any given moment. The amount of time this process will take is in direct proportion to the amount of patience and surrender to attachment to the physical form that we need to go through. From this perspective, the process is perfect, and the resulting gift is humility, freedom and love for our true nature.

You mean that I ought to surrender to this duality in order to move beyond it?

I suggest that you surrender to the mechanics of this process via an act of trust that it is being overseen by a higher intelligence. This surrender to the intelligence of our true self unlocks a sense of safety and the wisdom that we are actually always living in the right moment. Just look out across the sky and know that whatever is looking back at you brought you here out of love, and it would never impose anything else upon you. Embrace with curiosity the parts of you that wonder; it's a sign of love for your true self. Also know that you will look back on this moment with laughter and tears in your eyes.

Impulsivity and Patience

When we get a visit from our energetic guests from the past, in the present moment, we ought to embrace and welcome them with love. This will move us into another important shift in how we authentically navigate life by removal of dysfunctional impulsivity from our life experience. Impulsivity is the unconscious movement of attention by firstly assigning the underlying energy another meaning and then rapidly adding a behavioral movement and additional activities. Human beings call this being a "restless soul," but the more appropriate name is a mentally created escape-route-via-activity, in order to escape energies in the present moment.

Impulsivity's core driver is flight. In this setting, impulsivity is the same as being impatient with ourselves, and it has its roots in energies that go along with fear and frustration, which is the same as fearful anger. When we don't know how to digest these energies within the present moment and draw wisdom from the insight, we project them outwardly and indulge in various activities.

Even if the activities have a genuine intention, like helping others or working, the root cause still has its base in an escape from the present moment, and hence will at some point disappoint us heavily. We refer to impulsivities underlying the energetic state as restlessness, and only an unconscious mind can have this experience. Impulsivity is also highly addictive since, although these are the same energetic states that are present when we have an experience of fear and anxiety, in the mentally premature context of impulsivity we call it excitement. In other words, when we state that we enjoy excitement and impulsivity, we are stating that we are addicted to the restless states of fear and anger.

Once we anchor ourselves within our inner body, we feel these energetic paradoxes that we typically find to be uncomfortable. We move beyond all impulsivity by not buying into the mental body's narrative that wants to drive us into activity-based action by firstly agreeing to be still. Agreeing to feel our inner perceived storm strengthens one of the most important muscles of life: *patience*. Practicing patience, which is the same as practicing present moment awareness, is the highest level of service we can perform in order to practice love for our true self – which is the same as practicing love for all others. Furthermore, when in our own experience we realize that one of the qualities of what we are, the pure awareness, is eternal and whole in itself, hurrying somewhere just becomes humorous.

What's the meaning of just being uncomfortable when I can shift this energy?

The meaning of this uncomfortableness is monumental since it will catapult you into the most powerful expression that you ought to express in this life. It is the same as saving yourself, and therefore others, from monumental suffering and confusion when you go inwards in order to operate on the most powerful side of your true self. When we agree to be with our restlessness, we gradually move up from the basement into the penthouse of life. That work is undoubtedly worth the view to come. Furthermore, no one is asking us to sit down and be miserable. This energy can find its outlet in creative forms of movement such as painting, walking and dancing.

This just makes me feel lazy when I could be doing something productive with this energy.

This statement has primarily a generational, cultural and social imprinting around the definition of productivity that is entangled with the unconditional energetic qualities of your true being. It is vital to untangle these two – that is, not to identify our true nature with productivity – in order to feel peace. On the level of doing, productivity is a result-based activity that is quantified and measurable. It's conditional energy in a box. Productivity is best left for robots. We are human beings; our true core is the unconditional energy field, which operates in a higher energetic field that allows us to create from our shared Being. We are *created to be creative* and preferably not to restrict energies, which leads to both unbalance and suffering in our life experience. This is also why we can creatively build robots to do repetitive, measurable tasks with far higher productivity than we could demonstrate. We can't afford to mix the definition of productivity with that of creativity; therefore, when restless, we remain still in order to draw wisdom, and then in our present moment experience the difference. When the difference is known, you will achieve extraordinary productivity within your creativity that is in line with your life's purpose.

Dying to Know
– Resolution of the Illusion of Death

From the very second each one of us opened our eyes and got our first sight and perception of the world, we embarked on a journey towards the essential need to know who we are, why we are here and where we came from. Since we have left the absolute joy and peace of consciousness, it's a traumatic experience for our true being to come into the conditional context of a human-constructed life experience. On one level, we left what we absolutely loved the most in order to take on a human life form.

This is absolutely contrary to what we are later taught and imprinted with: that we should cherish life and avoid at all costs what we refer to as death. We think, feel and act fearfully around all topics regarding death and the journey into the unknown. Therefore, we have a responsibility to put this ancient imprinting to rest and come to a resolution with death by surrendering to the experience of *dying to know and dwell in the unknown*. This fearful imprinting creates an immense amount of suffering and disharmony in our life experience since we are, on various levels, driven to entertain a level of unconsciousness based on fear when we run away from the topic of death. We ought to solve this human-constructed puzzle in our own experience.

Furthermore, if left unresolved, the concept of death drives us into endless action, fighting all sorts of diseases in order to try to prolong this human life experience and trying to find the biggest cause of death. On that level, we actually already know the biggest cause of death: birth. Therefore, the only way not to physically die is to avoid birth in the first place. However, since we are already physically here in a human expression, and you are reading these lines, that is not a realistic option nor the ultimate wisdom. Therefore, we surrender to the experience of the present moment that will dissolve the illusion of death – instantly.

Typically, when human beings refer to death, we mean the dissolving of our organism, or our physical body. We rarely bother to ask the deeper layer of ourselves where we were before we knew that we were physically alive, not to mention the important question of how we even know that we exist. If we wish to find peace and eternal joy in life, we can't afford to hold imprinted and inherited concepts, like the concept of death, without finding out in our own experience if there even is such an experience as death.

You're suggesting that death doesn't exist?

Human beings are imprinted to refer to things as "real" only within the small view and limitations of our human frequency of experience. Your experience only exists because you are interacting with it. When you discover who this *you* who is interacting with all these experiences is, you will discover that the human-constructed concept of death doesn't exist simply because this *you*, who is aware of all these experiences, could never, nor will ever have an experience of non-existing. In this sense, if death is the awareness of the existence of non-existence, you will never have that experience, and therefore, such a death can't exist.

I can't relate to this statement nor to an experience of non-existence.

Just like the concept of death, that is because there is no such experience. One way to broaden our perspective here is to consider the experience of sleep. You fall asleep every night and go into another frequency of human experience, which is, from a consciousness perspective, broader or less limiting than our daily experience. In your sleep, you have a totally different experience and knowledge of your body and ability to interact with your experience, which we often refer to as our dreams.

When we wake up, we are able to contain memories of our dreams and state the quality of our sleep. This is pure evidence, within our own frequent experience, that something is aware of us being aware that we are sleeping. From that perspective, the human-constructed concept of death has the same reality as everyday sleep. Hence, death is just another moment of fully embracing the present moment as you surrender to what is, into the unknown. This is also an undoubtable truth about every breath we take. Every breath is a good breath to die for.

I am considering embarking on this journey and resolving the illusion of death when I get time in my life.

You are already on this journey. As soon as a human being is born, they are on a journey home. Therefore, directly upon birth we embark on a quest to be willing and prepared to do anything to know who we are. This is life, or existence, by design, and no one can escape this truth. Human beings have an absolute imbedded necessity to know.

We basically have two options once we become adults. One is to embark on the journey consciously by applying our free will in order to reach the highest potential of our form; the second is to allow ourselves to be thrown around in life unconsciously by reacting to other bodies' energy fields and imprinting, which leaves us in despair, confusion and suffering. The natural consequences and limitations of dwelling in a human form will always manifest, no matter our choice. Either we choose peace by responding throughout these experiences, or we choose to react and suffer in drama. Since our Being loves us unconditionally, it will never force any of these choices upon us.

I understand this intellectually, but I am still afraid of dying.

This statement has a duality imbedded within itself. Duality is the same as two opposites, and two opposites are the same as conflict. All conflict creates friction within our field of awareness, and friction creates confusion. In order to settle this confusion, we need to dismantle this statement. A statement like "I understand this intellectually, but…" is a tool of the mental body that seems to initially agree, then counter-strikes with a "but," which is pure disagreement. This is the mental body's attempt to gain control over the unknown by creating a new conflict of polarities that leaves us entrapped in psychological fear. Left unresolved, this statement, or core belief, leaves a trace of unresolved anxiety and unsafety in our life experience.

We dismantle this belief by recognizing the difference between biological fear, on the level of the body's instinct to protect itself and survive, and the mental body's narrative about this experience. Both of these are unlocked by simply embracing the present moment, as it is. Our physical body can experience intense shaking and sweating from biological fear while we simultaneously have a completely calm and sorted mental body.

So, how do I move beyond the concept of death and the biological fears?

Firstly, when we go into our inner body, we gather wisdom that the biological fear is an illusion since we know from experience that higher intelligence will kick in in the present moment when needed. A good example is when we are about to stumble; our being kicks in and does its utmost to neutralize the fall by activating the required bodily movement. We don't go around thinking about falling. Similarly, when we are sick, all of our cells gather energy in an incredible way to fight the infection. We simply surrender to this experience and trust that harmony will manifest as needed. Most of our inner body reactions are enforced by a restless mental body that wears our nervous system down to a reaction. These mechanics run their course to completion until we have organically detached from our ego. Lastly, it's the mental body's story about death that we have absorbed by listening to others, and based on this confusing story, we build a lifelong attachment to the external form. We start the dissolution of this attachment by asking the question: Was I, before my birth, missing anything or afraid of anything? We then feel, in the present moment, the wholeness and safety in our Being. We feel the truth that we are actually safe everywhere and always.

Grief is Wisdom

Along the Road

I walked a mile with Pleasure;
She chatted all the way;
But left me none the wiser
For all she had to say.

I walked a mile with Sorrow;
And ne'er a word said she;
But, oh! The things I learned from her,
When Sorrow walked with me.

–Robert Browning

One of the most honest phenomena in the human life experience is grief, but most human beings overlook its true potential by suppressing, distracting, and camouflaging these states. We ought to follow our griefs, since the wisdom they contain will never lie to us. Pleasure is seductive, while grief is always clear and honest. Therefore, following the path of our griefs is following an accelerated path towards the truth.

Grief can be defined as all the contradictory physical, mental and emotional dimensions we may encounter within our field of awareness about a perceived loss and change. An additional definition of grief is letting go of a past or a future that we will never have. It's fundamental to recognize that the dissolution of the personalized self, or the ego, is equally a set of griefs. We mourn our old beliefs and consequences. When we embrace our social, cultural, and generational imprinting, we encounter the experience of grief. This may manifest subtly for some, while others may experience a more acute reaction that resonates with a life crisis, and that life, as they knew it, falls apart. It's more accurate to state that true life, our true self, *is falling into place*. Nevertheless, grief ought to be honored and embraced in the present moment as we gently dismantle the physical sensations, thoughts, and feelings of what we are not.

Furthermore, all change is grief. Every breath is a small death, and every small death is a small grief. This leaves us on a collective level with an underlying sense of accumulated sorrow. On that level, human beings are deeply sad since all of us will eventually lose everything we love and care for. This accumulated collective sorrow intensifies the personal narratives about our life experiences and strengthens the separation. Therefore, grief needs to be deeply examined if one wants to truly live. If we are present enough, we will notice that beneath the surface, every conversation on a personal level carries a sense of sorrow. We all acknowledge that even "happy" conversations and experiences will eventually end.

On a personal level, grief is an intensified sense of discontinuity, a perceived loss and, if not consciously addressed, the root of all sorts of fear, separation, and conflict, both internally and externally. Grief is a mind and body earthquake of a well-known pattern of images. Our attachment to the physical form also intensifies our grief reaction through a mind state based on the belief that we have somehow missed or lost something of authentic value. The human physical reaction that frees us from grief is simply crying. Depending on how present we are, our reactions to grief may manifest in different forms. Grief is a set of physical sensations, thoughts and feelings that accompanies a loss or a change. It's neither necessary nor beneficial to name all these states, although it's vital to acknowledge that grief cluster reactions very much include states of fear and anger before we tap into the joy of tears.

The intention of conscious grieving is not to try to forget a loss, since this will merely strengthen the images and sensations. The authentic intention with grieving is to embrace and honor all dimensions of our loss, no matter how others may perceive the importance of this particular loss. The validity of the loss can only be defined by the importance and intensity it has for our own life experience. Therefore, grief is mostly an internal set of agreements that we ought to dissolve in our own life experience. Only by fully embracing all physical sensations, thoughts and feelings in the grace of the present moment will we put all grief to rest. The noble way to embrace grief is to consciously acknowledge and let these waves come into our experience in order to be comforted as a part of the whole. By grieving, we set ourselves free, both from narratives and from the pressure of our charged inner body. These tears are the water of wisdom about what life truly is. In practice, this is how we demonstrate love towards the form we cherished in this life experience.

There's so much I wanted to say to my loved ones before they suddenly died. What can I do?

I suggest that you say those things to them now. Human beings are largely and deeply imprinted with an urge to complete communication verbally before we can reach completion on a mental level. Further, we are to a large extent imprinted with the idea that this communication needs to be heard by another individual in order to be valid or approved. Humans have entertained the experience of confession for centuries in order to solve this dilemma. Therefore, we honor our predicament and follow this inclination in order to set ourselves free from mental conflict so that we can let these waves run their course on the level of our inner body experience. We can simply write a letter to the person, belief or object that we feel we have lost and read it to a conscious person in order to complete the communication. We ought to engage in a conscious intention to forgive ourselves and others if we truly want to embrace and dissolve the experience of grief. This is typically necessary as long as we identify with the narratives that bind the underlying pressure of emotions. Once awakened, we are simply in the midst of grief. Right here, right now.

This is quite a simple way of looking at something as complex as grief.

This is a belief that the ego loves to entertain: that life must be harder. We have all kinds of false imprinting around shame, guilt and mental images that "time will heal all wounds." Elapsed time may give room for more experiences to flow through our field of awareness, which may result in a broader perspective, but more experiences alone can't solve our conflicts. However, what does solve all conflicts is embracing our physical sensations, thoughts and feelings honestly and unconditionally by observing them – observing all the rich aspects of the human experience of loss, with curiosity and depth. The mechanisms of our being are utterly simple; they become complex when we condition them. We consider and assign all sorts of inaccurate and unexplored attributes to different experiences and then box them into a timeframe. Thereafter, we become angry and enter a conflict about the fact that they are in a box and don't behave according to our imprinted expectations. A hint is that we put them there by collectively absorbing what we believe to be true without examining this paradigm in our own experience. Therefore, we consciously grieve in order to *know* what grief truly is.

What is the accurate way of looking at grief, then?

It's more accurate to view grief as an intimate celebration of life – a dedicated time in our life experience when we are given the opportunity to transform and grow. Forms come to an end when the end is most necessary; the question is whether we are willing to grow into the deep wisdom and meaning behind the physical form by responding to these experiences. Grief has a unique gift that uncovers what we truly are, honestly and clearly.

When will all this grief be over?

When you no longer have the need to entertain this question.

Beyond Groups and Concepts

It's not necessary to *join* or to identify ourselves with any form of human-constructed group. Creating and maintaining subgroups based on concepts such as beliefs, families, corporations, religions or nations is a result of ancient attempts to control unconscious behavior and bring a security that originally had roots in a sense of unsafety and confusion – which is the same as fear. This fear may continue to drive all sorts of aggressive and separatist behavior if not explored consciously.

The collective fear within a group is usually controlled by maintaining a collective narrative that aims to hold the group together. Since the narratives are based on fear, they are highly conditional and exclusive. Structuring subgroups within the human experience, and thereafter identifying with them as a concept in order to feel that there is predictability and safety in this world, will not settle our inner conflict of existential fear if these concepts are not examined thoroughly as a state of being within our own experience. Concepts and groups alone will not lead us home to God if we don't *feel* in touch with the personal God within. Even if a group or a concept sporadically gives us a sense of comfort, over time we are at risk of becoming disappointed and discouraged if we don't take responsibility. This type of disappointment often manifests as experiences of crisis, such as "the dark night of the soul," deep states of anger, and blaming "God" for abandoning and failing us. Naturally, this accumulated anger was already in us; we have only temporarily transferred it collectively onto the group or covered it up with a concept. We then have the opportunity to forgive ourselves and others and truly live the qualities of the Divine. Only then can we truly *be in the group, but not of the group.*

Simultaneously, it's neither necessary nor beneficial to *leave* any form of a group by maintaining a new belief, an exile identity. We can simply watch ourselves *Being* born into a religious experience on a personal level. Like all experience, this is a part of our journey and ought to be experienced and examined. At the heart of all religions, we will find the truth. And truth we must seek if we want to be religious.

On a larger level, we are already a part of a group in the form of the species called human beings. In that sense, the whole world is our family and ought to be treated accordingly. Bringing about harmony within the family is bringing about harmony within our own experience and journey. This is what *Being* religious is all about. Unexplored beliefs and concepts create duality and conflict on various levels of our being when we identify with them. We can't be at peace if we maintain and identify with any concepts or images that are not explored and true in our life experience. Unfortunately, there are no exceptions to this rule.

PART III

BEING YOURSELF

Movement within eternity

Re-entrance into Experience of the World

Like all circles of eternity, the journey home is not finalized before we re-enter the world by re-entering and responding to the experience of our worldly destiny. However, we now enter the experience of the world with a universal remedy. As shown by the order of the term *human being*, we enter the experience of our being *through* our human form, and never around it. All such endeavors, even if they are a necessity in order for deeper surrender to occur, are nevertheless sidetracks to our path home. Our humanness is our vehicle and expression of our shared Being. We ought to embrace it and have fun with this expression in this human experience. At this stage, our main prayer is as a state of being in this world. We simply pray for more truth while we are in the truth. Now, we are not just open but curious about all manifestations of this truth. We are grateful for the experience of life. At this stage, our eyes are always open in any meditative practice, and we become the masters of life. The way we operate in the world is the meditation and prayer itself.

Once we have gathered, by feeling-knowing experience, the simple wisdom of who we are, we are ready to move beyond knowing ourselves into being ourselves. This is the part of the journey where we embrace the new lofty us by responding to the expression we ought to be in this world. This is also the part of the journey where we discover how to navigate and respond to our experience throughout all levels of our being. At this leg of the journey, we are stepping out in the world with a new universal tool and wisdom about who we are. We are ready to, through experience, discover and balance the energies and the wisdom of *being in the world, but not of the world.*

It is not uncommon for our shared Being to rearrange our social groups in order to align us with our true purpose. If this is the case, we ought to respond to this call by moving intentionally towards energy fields that have proven to be authentic. Now is the time to consciously ask questions to Being while we are in the midst of the experience in order to experience the true qualities of our Being. Thereafter, we ought to implement this wisdom in the midst of the experience to come as an intimate part of our present moment.

My experience is still clouded occasionally by inner body contractions.

This is a natural unfolding and movement towards the interest of your true self, beyond the intensity and content of perceptions and sensations. We move beyond by moving our attention from the perceived chaos of the egoistic death into the curiosity of what rebirth into eternity will bring. If the storm is heavy, connect with your breathing until you get in touch with your inner body; sit gently in the boat and enjoy the ride until a lull emerges. There's no need to hurry or to create further confusing energetic movement by asking conflicting questions to Being while the intensity of the experience is high.

It's more beneficial to anchor ourselves in the present moment until the sky is clearer. We get exactly what we need in order to gather the necessary wisdom from that particular present moment. Stay true to the present moment and respond consciously to what is by asking the question: In this moment, what does patience look like? Then simply be the quality of patience.

Others tell me that I don't have empathy after my awakening.

Most human beings are imprinted with the false belief that empathy is physically, mentally, and emotionally modeling others at the same intensity level in order for the response to be valid. We are even taught that this type of drama is an act of love. Although this is an imprinted belief, we can still respond to lower-level energies consciously by having respect for other individuals' misunderstanding of our journey. Simply non-judgmentally embrace that they are now, just like us, where they ought to be. Intuitively responding to the present moment with silence is the highest form of both empathy and sympathy. Stay true to the present moment and respond consciously to what is by asking the question: In this moment, what unites us? Then simply be the quality of unity.

It's so confusing to relate to the external world after my awakening when I know that I am not the world.

It is not enough to know what we are not since our subconscious doesn't understand negations. Therefore, we ought to consciously ask what we are and, based on that discovery, simply be that. You might experience difficulties in responding to other individuals' feelings or behaviors on the level of personal form once you have dismantled your narratives and integrated the underlying charged energy within the inner body.

This is a natural and healthy unfolding of your soul at this leg of the journey. When you embrace the present moment, the new lofty you will intuitively fall into place within your field of awareness. Stay true to the present moment and respond consciously to what is by asking the question: In this moment, what is my human expression called to be? Then simply be the qualities of that expression.

Revealing Your Purpose and Meaning

While we are living in time, where our attention is almost exclusively given to the high-pitched predicament of external activities and the devastating belief that we are these activities and objects, we think that our purpose is something we need to find. We get entangled in the details and drama of life in the form that is operating on the level of cause and effect. We then do our utmost to gather evidence from clusters of unfinished physical, mental and emotional circumstances from the past in order to find some sort of meaning around the purpose of us being here.

Firstly, we need to recognize the conflict of approaching this paradigm in this way and why it has failed us to this point. The fact that we haven't yet figured this out has nothing to do with our intelligence. It has to do with a greater scheme of life where our form has not been ready, up to this point, to reveal its true potential. There is deeper purpose and harmony for the whole in how our journey is evolving.

Most human beings are imprinted that the meaning of *our being* is found *in doing*. This is highly enforced imprinting, starting from our childhood, when we are constantly asked: "What will you do when you grow up?" But the mechanism of our being is just the opposite. As children, we are quite awakened, and when we scan our life to that point, we answer the question from the correct, casual point of enthusiasm and joy. As children, we simply and quietly ask ourselves internally, "What gives my being great joy and enthusiasm?" Thereafter, we scan our surroundings and memories of when we encountered this state of our true nature. We then ask, "When did my being feel full of enthusiasm, oneness, joy, and presence?" We may connect that state of being to an experience of playing football with our friends. We then reply, "I want to be a football player!" Note that we always state what we want to *be* first; we never state what we want to *do* first. In that sense, we never need to find what we want to do, but we need to reveal what we want to be.

Since we are already born with a set of gifts and talents whereby our form thrives on its full potential, it's not an activity of finding a doing, but mainly revealing a state of being. Within, in a deeper level of ourselves, we already know what we ought to be in this world. We usually feel this strongly when we are in a state of being inspired. There, if just for a split second, we reveal just what we ought to be in our true Being.

For the vast majority of human beings, these revelations usually occur in short windows, just before our mental body, social and cultural imprinting, and limiting beliefs around adulthood counterstrike with fear. We then withdraw to the prison of mental body and state that we don't know and that we are confused. We ought to stop this unconscious behavior by realizing that the mental body is the wrong tool for revealing our true purpose. The mental body can assist us at a later stage in the *what and how* by consciously steering our attention, but never in the deeper being of *why*. Therefore, we need to reveal our true purpose and meaning in order to be in alignment with our form and enter the heavens of fulfillment.

How should I reveal my purpose?

You have been in touch with your purpose your whole life, even if you haven't acknowledged it due to imprinting, unconsciousness, and the drama of activities. Our purpose can only be revealed in the present moment, and it requires us to slow down until we can be in touch with this gift. It also involves us operating from the functional part of our true self with patience until we are conscious enough to sincerely be responsible. Since our purpose has great power, it also has imbedded within it great responsibility before it is fully revealed to us. Our purpose is simply the influence we have in other individuals' lives when we are in alignment with our Being. The specific gifts and talents your expression carries will be revealed by scanning your life experience and asking the question: When have I felt truly inspired, and how did it make others feel? Your purpose is the state of being that they describe, which is the same state of being that you will feel.

What's your purpose, then?

My expression feels deeply alive when I share the qualities of our shared Being while other individuals simultaneously state that they feel inspired in that present moment. My purpose is simply then to inspire others to find their truth, which is the same as their purpose. A simpler way to address this is that my purpose is simply to be present. As evident in this statement, or more importantly in the experience itself, the levels merge; my human expression and my beingness meet in oneness. They are not two.

How should I outline the meaning of my expression in life?

Meaning is the higher consequence for the whole which comes through being, and living, your purpose. It is the great good when we serve our Being by being present, so to speak.

What is your meaning, then?

The consequence of inspiring others to find their truth is simply freedom, peace and joy. Since it brings joy to you, it simultaneously brings joy to me. This is the same as fulfillment, which is the same as responding to the true expression our forms are meant to take. This brings harmony within the state of being for everyone who touches it.

What is the pathway to my purpose and meaning?

Firstly, there are no other activities or predicaments outside our everyday life that ought to occur in order for us to reveal our soul's purpose and meaning. Both purpose and meaning are revealed in the simplicity of ordinary everyday life – never in the ego's dreams or illusions about the extraordinary. We ought to fully commit to the present moment with the intention of revealing our purpose, and both our purpose and meaning will be revealed at just the right time. The movement of our intention will manifest experiences, places, circumstances, and individuals to support this quest. We ought to consciously state, express and behave in accordance with this quest until our purpose is synchronized and true in our own life experience. Our task is to listen and follow with courage since the whole universe is now lined up to support this purpose purposely. Thereafter, life will automatically call us to live our purpose and meaning through the way the doing, or the *how* and *what* of life, is shown. All doings are simply there to enforce a fulfilled state of being. All doings are therefore a response to the true nature of our Being. Doing then becomes just a dance and a celebration of life itself, regardless of what we do.

Being Your Purpose and Meaning

As the saying goes – *when the path to God ends, the path within God begins.* The final leg of our journey home to eternity is resting in the beginning of eternity itself. We rest in our Being as we rest in the shadows of the present moment. This is the time when we are called to surrender to the joy of life and learn, through our own experience, what joy is.

While initial peace is delightful compared to a shell-shocked mind, we ought to surrender and continue on our path to the dynamic dimension of peace – which is joy. Just as no one can give us authentic peace, no one can surrender to joy for us. This is the time when we ought to respond and surrender in totality to life itself and the purpose for which we are here. This is the time when we explore our talents and gifts by getting in touch with our creativity. We then share this creativity unconditionally with the world in order to be of service. We respond by being responsible and taking the position in the circle of life we are called to take. We don't create further habitual mental drama that keeps us in the parking lot by dwelling on how this journey will look. We simply take the journey – now.

We also recognize that on the level of form, things are constantly changing, and that it will constantly be on some dimension that, if we catch a glimpse, will look like we ought to sacrifice something in order to live our purpose. We want to meet and embrace this belief of the last sacrifices and accompanying consequences with full commitment to the wisdom of our soul. We now know that whatever is unfolding is absolutely crucial for our form to take its full potential. Especially when the terrain is rough and habitual mental body patterns occur, we must hold steadfast to our intention. Then we step into the power of the present moment, which makes us absolutely unstoppable. We don't let the shadows of old imprinting or limiting beliefs stop anything that ought to move, nor force anything to move that ought to be still. We step into the fearlessness of our shared Being and set a bulletproof intention to which we surrender.

What should I do to avoid being stuck in the parking lot?

We surrender to the process of discovery by experience. If we go out into the experience of life, we will be shown our calling. Simultaneously, we should be delicate in terms of the energetic commitment we initially invest in order to discover that calling. Everything starts small, and we must surrender to the process of being beginners in the present moment. Just know, now, that everything will be given at exactly the right place, pace and moment.

Life doesn't seem to be showing me any particular calling yet.

You are then being prepared to live your purpose by deepening of the present moment. Your calling requires deep wisdom and patience. The intensity of your awakening and your predicament in prior unconsciousness states are important dimensions and experiences that will reveal your purpose. Nothing, absolutely nothing, from the moment we are born until the last breath we are given, happens by coincidence. If you approach the totality of these experiences, you will clearly see a holistic purpose. Your responsibility is to respond, wherever you are currently, in order to support your soul's will. This is done by first revealing and then being this purpose – purposely.

I feel it's hard to navigate and plan now when I don't live in time.

This statement has its roots in habitual and socially acceptable limiting beliefs that stem from time itself. We break these chains by recognizing the fatality of these illusions, which are based on fears around a made-up future that are then projected onto the present moment. Firstly, planning is always done in the present moment. Secondly, planning is not mentally escaping to images of what might or might not happen around the planned activity. Planning is not the same as knowing or expecting that the planned activity will actually occur. No one knows the actual outcome. Planning is a vision and not a goal. It is also a journey, and not knowing the outcome is the beauty of a plan. When we enter the joy of life's surprises, we start to love our plans.

Enjoy Your Life

My parting gift to you is the simple reminder to truly, deeply and immensely enjoy your life! Naturally, in practice, this is the same as truly, deeply and immensely enjoying every moment. Enjoy the totality of it without getting overly consumed by any of it. This includes our love for the truth. None of this is a serious matter for our shared Being. We are all already whole in our pure quest, right here, right now. When we truly know that we are not our experience, and that we will sooner or later drop all our attachments to the present experience, we can simply agree to drop it now. Yes, we may encounter old habitual traits of physical aches, thoughts, or emotions throughout our human journey, but we now have a deeper wisdom about who we are. And since we have an eternity at our disposal, there's no hurry to dissolve it all at once.

Remember to laugh, a lot, and then more. Nothing breaks the perceived veil and the egoistic traits as quickly as deep, authentic laughter at situations that we have been conditioned to react to as if they were serious matters. Simply let life be life. Nothing more, and nothing less.

In the next section, I have gathered insights from my own experience regarding the topics of frequently asked questions. The pure intention is to address the main barriers and to activate authentic movement in you to follow your expression's purpose. The structure and the amount of textual content is intentionally minimized in order to not disturb your own exploration within your life experience.

Peace Through Neutrality

In order to rest in our true self, it's vital to consciously intend to explore what peace is within our own experience by consciously being peace in this world. When we are awakened, we are also acutely aware of both our own and others' manifestations of mind traits. This heightened level of consciousness carries a great responsibility when we navigate our life experience going forward.

This is the ability to respond with peace when observing ourselves and others. It is the same as responding non-judgmentally, gently and with compassion. This doesn't mean carrying around a mental image about peace and intentionally being overly nice to everyone or doing things that we are not destined to do. Nor does it mean that we interrupt others' experiences in the world that they ought to go through in order to be awakened. Uncovering others' mind traits without their consent can create unnecessary disturbance and drama and be a traumatic shift in the life experience of that individual. This creates disturbance for the whole, which is the opposite of peace. Being responds perfectly to any quest, but everyone needs to consent by consciously making the request. No one can prescribe this request for anyone else, and without consent, no good deed goes unpunished. Furthermore, even when we are authentically declining an activity or offer, we do so with peace. Peace is simply responding to life with a gentle neutrality.

Since we are now increasingly dwelling in pure awareness, we ought to be wide awake and not to fall for egoistic bounces where heightened awareness is misused. An utterly simple example is that we don't judge ourselves or others due to the fact that we are now aware of most of the content in our field of awareness. When this occurs, we put our awareness on the awareness itself. In practice, we put attention on our breathing and inner body experience until we are anchored in the shadows of the present moment again. We also ought to continue the exploration of our experience honestly and deeply until we can sincerely contain the wisdom that peace has nothing to do with whether a mind is calm or not. A calm mind, or a mind empty of perceived turbulent content, can lack peace, just as a mind with heightened intensity can feel deep peace. Hence, the peace is in the experiential wisdom that we are not our mind. Peace is the gift we give ourselves for not entering into conflict with the present moment.

Service and Helping Others

Awakened beings don't need to carry any preconceived ideas about laws or beliefs since the pure quality of our true selves is perfect harmony. Awakened beings don't distract themselves by carrying mental images of what helping others means. This has nothing to do with any mental images or past beliefs around "the right thing to do" since there's no universal truth to such phenomena that can be extracted from the mental realm. Such truth can only be extracted from the totality of our beingness.

Awakened beings recognize that the highest service is to love themselves by being themselves. There's not a single activity in this world that anyone needs to do for anybody that is based on a must. When we awaken, we remove the sentence "I must..." from our life experience. We must only be ourselves, and that is not a must in itself since our true self is unconditionally generous by giving us opportunity to navigate our experience based on our free will. Free will is therefore the opposite of any musts. That's evidence enough, in our own experience, that there are no musts in this world. Therefore, we move from "I must" to the purely authentic energetic movement of "I want." *If we don't want, we don't must.* This is our birthright. All service ought to come from the seamless flow of truth that is extracted from the depth of the present moment. Nothing ought to be pushed that is destined to stay put and nothing ought to be stopped that is destined to move.

When we are in touch with ourselves, we can't intentionally hurt anyone. This doesn't mean that others can't have an egoistic narrative about how we should behave based in their ancient beliefs, but we needn't get concerned about such matters. We respond as gently as the present moment requires.

This brings justice to the present moment. Our pure intention is to be deeply present, and we will intuitively know the right course of action, right here and right now. Furthermore, after we awaken to our true self, we typically experience less need for particular activities or social gatherings to occur in order to feel that we are having fun. Being present is the ultimate fun. We move from activities where the intention was to prove that we are enough to simply being enough. This present moment is always enough. When we are in touch with ourselves, we are already complete and whole in this moment. This movement is both a healthy and natural development of our soul. It may initially manifest in such a way that we decline offers that we would have previously enjoyed, and a new baseline is revealed regarding what we authentically enjoy beyond previous imprinting.

Since the quality of our shared Being is oneness, there's only one act of service that we sincerely ought to give to this world: the service of being ourselves and responding to our true expression in this world by embracing every moment as equally important. Some of us who used to work directly with altruistic endeavors may notice a shift towards activities that have a deeper base in solitude and art. We are now of service by sharing our gifts through other channels and forms. Others, who were in what they may have perceived to be self-serving structures before awakening, may notice a broader shift in opportunities for service through their transformation. They may not feel inclined to move anywhere, since the internal movement is authentically bringing peace to everyone where they are. The journey onwards in terms of external acts of service manifests differently for every life expression, and your only responsibility is to respond to yours. Nothing more, but also nothing less.

Business and Money

Firstly, money is neither good nor bad. Money simply is. In our world, money is the most common currency we use to share energies. Money, when approached consciously, is liberating in that we can use it to navigate our life experience by energetic exchange in order to benefit everyone's true expression. We can receive and redirect the energy of money, so it benefits our surroundings in a wonderful manner. The fundamental purpose with any energy in the universe is to bring harmony and freedom. This is also true for the energy we call money.

However, in order to bring harmony to this energy, we ought to consciously embrace both our egoistic and imprinted false beliefs and narratives about money in order to feel authentically secured and abundant. Because large parts of our world are obsessed with assigning false meanings to different energy states, especially around money, this statement can't be emphasized enough. We ought to examine these false beliefs deeply and recognize and appoint correct meaning to money in our life experience in order to be free.

Awakening to our true self is also an energetic shift in terms of how we approach the energetic field of money. While we previously may have had a relationship with money based on egoistic beliefs of lack, we now move towards a more compassionate relationship based on wholeness and trust. We stop fear-based activities and impulsive risk-taking where the core driving force is a sense of lack. We stop accumulating funds with the intention of feeling superior or secure as we simultaneously recognize that we can very well have a lot of money and live a consciously beautiful life experience. This means that we can just as well have the life experience of a highly conscious stockbroker as we can have the experience of an unconscious starving monk.

We start to approach money with compassion when we recognize this energy's true potential. Just like with any energy, we don't condemn money. We recognize that there's a larger scheme to life and that human beings currently need such a phenomenon. Our task is to refine our craft and then share it with the world by being it in the world. If we are gifted with a set of talents, we have the skillset and we are destined to handle larger amounts of this energy, we do so responsibly. Similarly, if we feel energetic blockages connected to money flow, we resolve them by taking responsibility in order to bring harmony and consistency to our flow of money. There's no right or wrong amount of money flow we should aim for, although we ought to respond to the surroundings within which we are destined to operate. This differs all over our planet. We ought simply to adjust our perception and manifestation until we are rich and abundant on all levels of our being.

Since awakening to our true self requires that we respond to and question all concepts, we naturally also explore the concept of what we previously referred to as our professional life. Whereas we previously aspired to a linear career, we now aspire to be our career. Awakening to authenticity is awakening to the oneness of life. This journey manifests in different shapes and forms in the external world for all of us, but the common denominator is that we break the chains of restricting energies of a hard commitment to time. It's traumatic for unconditional beings to operate within such a conditioned paradigm. Typically, our relationship with work changes and we begin looking for a vision-driven predicament that is in alignment with our true purpose in order to serve and simultaneously feel deep fulfillment in the present moment. We don't settle for anything less. What Being wants to manifest, no man can divide.

Hence, we don't allow others' concepts to get in the way of our true expression. We simply can't afford nor should we tolerate navigating in such a manner anymore. We now navigate from a base in our true self, with enthusiasm and creativity. Neither do we tolerate internal conflicts based on false beliefs that we can't have both meaningful work and massive compensation. We ought to find our true tribe and serve them with our gifts. Furthermore, we don't let our focus get caught up in fears and blocked energies by others who are not from our tribe. We can't afford spillage of energy on individuals who won't take responsibility for their own fears. We need this energy to serve those who are meant to be served by us. Those who are not a part of our tribe are simply put on our path to help us navigate towards our true tribe.

In order to fulfill our true purpose, it's not unusual to be called to start our own business. If this is our calling, we ought to respond to this call and embark on this journey consciously. We do so by setting a fearless and unbreakable intention and being an example of conscious entrepreneurship in this world. We take action to utilize the resources that are given. We ask for and develop the skillset we need to hone our craft. We learn how to serve and sell without attachment. We learn that serving and selling are not polarities; they are not two separate entities. We learn that the core quality of our Being is harmony.

In order to find harmony, an energetic exchange always needs to occur to bring about balance. Therefore, we do not aim to give away our services or wisdom without balancing this energy. We simply ought to seek to balance this energy, and the most common way to do this within the paradigm of business is to be paid for our services. Giving away energy creates unbalance and is not an authentic way of serving. Unbalance manifests as disinterest for the one receiving the energy and frustration or resentment for the one who is giving, or rather spilling, the energy. Furthermore, the one who receives the energy naturally can't value nor contain the wisdom when the individual has not given consent by committing to an energetic exchange via payment.

This also occurs when we price the energy of our services too low. We ought to respect ourselves and others by charging the energy we need to live a comfortable life. This is Being's way of trying to find balance, and we ought to respond to this call and bring balance by charging appropriately for our services. Serving with hard-earned wisdom has never nor will ever be free. It's both impossible and counterproductive for the harmony of the whole to occur in such a way. Monks work very hard for entire days in the monastery in order to balance the energy between food and wisdom. If we want to be a monk in the current worldly predicament, then we will need to charge what we need for ourselves, our family and overall to support our purpose in this human expression. There's no exception to this universal rule. Now is the time to reclaim what was always ours. Now is the time to fearlessly respond to your calling, to take the position you are meant to take in the circle of life and to respond consciously in all aspects of your life experience.

Conscious Intimacy

Once we awaken to our true self by transforming our relationship with the present moment, a deep sense of intimacy with all life forms follows. We feel a deep connection with everyone and everything within our field of awareness. We awaken to the purity, innocence, and sensitivity of our true self. We ought to celebrate this dimension by actively being an intimate part of life. Since the core quality of our shared Being is acknowledgment of oneness, we ought to behave in accordance with this truth.

On the level of form, human beings instinctively search for the completion of wholeness. We search for balance by connecting and creating deep social interactions with others. Just like all animals, we have an impulse to mate and are wired to take care of our family and our whole community as such. Therefore, we are both imprinted and have an instinctive drive to find a partner.

Intimate relationships, when approached consciously, are by far the most honest and clear predicament that will reveal our barriers, resistance and egoistic traits within the present moment. There's no other arena where we get the chance to face ourselves so broadly and directly. No matter how awakened we think we are, on an instinctive level, we search for this completion and celebration of life to occur. We ought to honor the possibilities and gifts of such an endeavor. This doesn't mean that we ought to push for intimate relationship by egoistic force based on a sense of lack; it simply means that we ought to honor the fact that intimate relationships are a celebration of life itself. We ought to be open to any possibilities of the unknown.

More often than not, our egoistic traits will create a narrative that we ought to take care of ourselves first and that there's no space for another on such a journey. On one level, this may be our current authentic truth, but we need to be utterly honest with ourselves when we make such a statement and carefully observe whether this is just another egoistic way of avoiding internal intimacy by avoiding intimacy in the external world. We access the truth about ourselves by accessing the perceived impact others, or the world, have on our life experience. It's not unusual upon awakening to avoid the totality of such an experience by "choosing" an island experience. Our previous endeavors in the intimate relationships department may have been based on lack and the idea that we need to find the "love of our life." We were simply searching for someone to give us a sense of peace and security by giving us attention. We didn't have the deep experience of taking care of our own emotional needs and the wisdom that our true self is unconditional love itself. Therefore, those endeavors throughout our life experience usually ended in what we refer to as abandonment or hurt, either as a result of our own actions or the other person's. But we don't let these previous unconscious experiences stop us from celebrating life and embracing a conscious openness to intimate relationships. It's never too late to have your first conscious kiss.

We now relate in a new manner, knowing that our true self can never be hurt by any experience. *No breakup can break us up.* Certainly, on the level of human form we may experience clusters of grief or other mind patterns, but we needn't be concerned by any of this in the present moment. We are open and conscious and ought to celebrate life itself by celebrating the gifts of intimate relationships. We swap the search for the love of our life for a life that is full of love.

This journey will manifest authentic movement differently for all of us depending on what our expression is destined to go through. Some of us will have an experience of marriage and the gift of bringing up children of Being. Others will have an authentic experience of growth by getting a divorce. Since we are now consciously navigating our life experience, we ought to respond to whatever our expression wants to express.

We stay, we move, and we enter present relationships based on the wisdom of our heart, but the common denominator is that our intimate relationships now are full of peace and harmony. Whenever disagreement arises, we strive instantly to repair the connection and restore present moment awareness with our partner. We are with individuals who have energetic and conscious alignment with our Being's expression and purpose. We share company with individuals who not only support but also effortlessly and lovingly celebrate our expression's true purpose. We grow together into the peace of eternity. We are humble, gentle, and generous. This journey may start with ourselves, but it always ends with being one with all.

Creativity and Playfulness

As we awaken, we naturally move towards our urge to play and be creative. We become true children of our Being. We look at the manmade bewilderment of adulthood with humor as we decide to play and navigate, childlike, onwards. Nothing is really important or serious from now on. We choose to have fun by being fun. Since our shared Being is the creator, we are creative when in touch with it. This is the time when we embark on the eternal journey of sharing and expressing our true self.

We may feel drawn to write poems or books, or to paint, sing and dance. Now is the time to reclaim your childhood through conscious playfulness. We share our endeavors and gifts by fearlessly dwelling in our being. Our response is to fully participate in the celebration of life. Whereas we previously thought, felt and behaved like visitors in this world, we are now deep participants.

In being, we are deeply in touch with the magnitude of importance our expression has in this world. Whereas we previously needed to entertain thought-based patterns of superiority or manufactured positivity, we now dwell in a natural sense of being right, safe and connected. The creative work to which we surrender has vast importance for the ones we are meant to serve with our company. We ought to respond to this calling and follow through with whatever is shown to be true for us.

There are no borders to what we can accomplish when we operate from our true self. The sky is only perceived to be the limit when we are on the ground. Once we take flight, we discover that beyond the sky comes space, and that space itself is eternal. Therefore, we simply take off by taking one small step right now. Be the space. As you are the space, we will meet, again and again, in the eternal play of life. Let's enjoy the ride.

~~THE END~~

THE ETERNAL BEGINNING